HOLLYWOOD, MAYFAIR AND ALL THAT JAZZ

HOLLYWOOD, MAYFAIR AND ALL THAT JAZZ

The Roy Fox Story

ROY FOX

Leslie Frewin of London

First published 1975 by
Leslie Frewin Publishers Limited,
Five Goodwin's Court,
Saint Martin's Lane,
London WC2N 4LL, England.

This book is set in Baskerville

Photoset, Printed and Bound by
Weatherby Woolnough, Sanders Road,
Wellingborough, Northants.

ISBN 0 85632 171 0

Contents

Foreword by R J Minney		11
1.	California Youth	15
2.	My 'Royal' Cornet	33
3.	The Next Step	43
4.	Girls	49
5.	Bands and Clubs	61
6.	'Whispering'	69
7.	My First Band	81
8.	Miami	89
9.	New York	97
10.	California Again	111
11.	Marriage	121
12.	Jean Harlow	145
13.	I Work for Fox Studios	159
14.	To London!	171
15.	Clubs and Kings	181
16.	Touring	189
17.	Back to the States	197
18.	Pinfire	203
19.	Australia	211
20.	The War Years in the States	215
21.	London Again	229
22.	Changes	233
23.	Now!	243

Illustrations

1. Me playing the trumpet with the Gus Arnheim band at the Cocoanut Grove, Hollywood, 1927 *(Austin Clegg)*
2. At the fashionable Monseigneur Night Club, London, 1931 *(Roy Fox Collection)*
3. Our instrumental line-up at the Monseigneur Night Club, 1931 *(Swaine: Roy Fox Collection)*
4. Our 'gang' at the Cafe Anglais, Leicester Square, London, 1932 *(Roy Fox Collection)*
5. The Mack Sennett Bathing Beauties with Ben Turpin on the sand at Santa Monica *(National Film Archive)*
6. Agora Cinema, Brussels, 1932 *(Roy Fox Collection)*
7. The Belgian Royal Family at the Royal Command Performance, 1932 *(Roy Fox Collection)*
8. Jean Harlow with Ben Lyon in *Hell's Angels,* 1928 *(National Film Archive)*
9. 'The Cubs' with me at the Kit-Kat Club, London, 1933 *(Wemyess Craigie)*
10. Dorothea . . . if only she could have remained like this . . . *(Roy Fox Collection)*
11. Joan Crawford in *Our Dancing Daughters* *(National Film Archive)*
12. With singer Peggy Dell at the Kit-Kat, 1933 *(Austin Clegg)*
13. My favourite picture of Jean Harlow taken during our romance *(National Film Archive)*
14. My good friend Ford Sterling with the Keystone Cops *(National Film Archive)*
15. Duke Ellington at the start of our friendship which I shall always treasure *(National Film Archive)*

16. Sophie Tucker was one of the first stars I worked with in the early days ... and one of the greatest *(National Film Archive)*

17. Pinfire, my racehorse *(Fox Photos Ltd)*

18. The Paul Whiteman 'Rhythm Boys', Bing Crosby, Al Rinker and Harry Baris *(National Film Archive)*

19. A bit of relaxation with some of my greyhounds at Wembley Stadium *(Syndication International)*

20. Kay Kimber *(Roy Fox Collection)*

21. Louis Armstrong ... a guy I like to remember for the good times we had together *(National Film Archive)*

22. Denny Dennis *(Austin Clegg)*

23. Al Bowlly *(Wemyess Craigie)*

24. Palace Ballroom, Douglas, Isle of Man on TT night ... over ten thousand dancers *(Austin Clegg)*

25. A youthful Frank Sinatra when we met in Glasgow at the Empire Theatre *(Roy Fox Collection)*

26. A totally unique photograph of some of the leading band-leaders of their day in their role as instrumentalists *(Roy Fox Collection)*

27. With Geraldo and Henry Hall *(Syndication International)*

28. Eileen O'Donnell *(Roy Fox Collection)*

29. Gary, my son *(Roy Fox Collection)*

30. Me today, 1975 *(Universal Pictorial Press & Agency)*

Acknowledgements

I would like to pay tribute to the members of my British bands who did their best to make our music the best in the land.

There was Syd Buckman and Jack Nathan, Maurice Burman and Ivor Mairants, Art Christmas and Les Lambert, Harry Gold, Rex Owen, Harry Balen, Jock Bain, Eric Tann, Hughie Tripp, Andy McDevitt, George Gibbs, George Rowe, Andy Hodgkiss and Arthur Bell, our arranger. Not forgetting, of course, Lew Stone, Bill Harty, Nat Gonella, Joe Ferrie, 'Tiny' Winters, Harry Berly, Billy Amstel, Ernest Ritte and Jim Easton.

And, in the post-war period: Victor Feldman, 'Tubby' Hayes, Lennie Bush, Tony Crombie, Benny Green, Martin Aston, Stan Tracy and others.

My vocalists included – aside from Syd Buckman, Nat Gonella and Joe Ferrie – Al Bowlly, Denny Dennis, Mary Lee, Bobby Joy, Peggy Dell, Jack Plant, Ronnie Genarder, Pat McCormick, Jack O'Hagan, Tony Mercer, Rose Brennan, Primrose, Barry Gray and 'The Cubs'.

And my grateful thanks to Wemyess Craigie whose undying interest in the band has kept all our fan club members supplied with the latest information for so many years (and still does!).

These were some of the people who by their efforts helped to make my stay in Britain a success and I remember with warmth the happy days we spent together. Some of these marvellous musicians are no longer with us but to them all – *many* thanks.

My grateful thanks, also, to B Feldman and Company of 138-140 Charing Cross Road, London WC2 for their permission to reproduce the first 3 bars of *Whispering*.

London 1975   *RF*

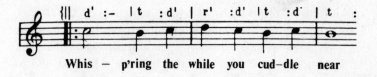

Whis — p'ring the while you cud–dle near

Foreword

MUSIC ENTERED ROY FOX'S life from the time of his birth in Denver, Colorado in 1901. Soon afterwards, his parents, who were in the Salvation Army, moved to Los Angeles, California, where their tambourines charmed his ears, pointed the way to his future and brought him worldwide fame.

He started young. At the age of three he sang the Salvation Army songs, and made his debut by standing on the big bass drum and singing *When the Roll is Called Up Yonder*. His knees kept knocking, but his singing was perfect.

At the age of eleven his career really began: pausing at the window of a second-hand store, he saw a bright nickel plated cornet which beckoned irresistibly. Priced at eleven dollars, it was quite beyond his reach, and beyond his mother's; but she kept turning it over in her mind and eventually got together enough money to buy it. Roy, beaming with joy on his way home, blew his very first blast and almost shattered all the neighbouring windows. An elderly German shoemaker taught him how to finger the valves and play the scales – 'that was really the extent of my musical education as a cornet player,' he says. They sat and played duets together in the backyard after the shoemaker shut his shop: some neighbours complained, but fortunately most of them did not.

As Roy's playing improved he was invited by a young couple to join their small orchestra in their parlour by way of a pleasant diversion: the wife, who played the piano, shortly afterwards persuaded him to bring his cornet to a movie house where she played the 'hurry' music when the train was about to run over the 'heroine' who was tied to the track, or to wring one's heart when the lovers were about to be parted. Roy was thrilled but the movie house was too far away. He soon found a Bijou Kinema nearer home and played his cornet there at week-ends and got all the tickets for the film shows for his family. At the age of thirteen he joined the Los Angeles Examiner Newsboys' Band: he liked to play the lead which provided the melody and he did it well. 'I was *always* nervous,' he said, 'even on the stage of the Palace Theatre on Broadway in New York City and at the Palladium in London' – but, even so, he got right to the very top quite early in his career.

He was still in his very early teens when Cecil B De Mille sent for him to play bugle calls in the film studio. The star was Gloria Swanson and Roy, despite his immaturity, fell madly in love with her. Girls played a big part in his life as you will see in this entertaining autobiography.

Some months later, when he was fifteen, he applied for work as a messenger boy in a bank: with the money he got from the bank he bought a new-style horn to take the place of his cornet, which he gave in part payment. After that the road was easy. He was invited to play in a very swanky restaurant in Los Angeles which was frequented by famous film stars. 'When I first saw William S Hart and Pauline Frederick come into the place to eat and dance to our music I was overawed.'

Then on to San Francisco. A very pretty young girl in a restaurant asked him to pass the sugar and later took him to her apartment to listen to her records and dance with her . . . it led to her teaching Roy 'what boys and girls were all about . . .' but he soon discovered that she was not the right kind of girl for him.

In the various clubs and restaurants where Roy's band played he met numerous celebrities, some of whom became close friends. They included the Marx Brothers: Harpo brought his harp and had delightful sessions with Roy. At a charity concert in New York as Roy walked off the stage a man came up to him and said: 'Hey, son. You are going to do all right with that horn of yours.' The speaker was Al Jolson, whose *The Jazz Singer* launched the talkies. Harold Lloyd, Buster Keaton, Charlie Chaplin, Rudolph Valentino, who tried to teach Roy how to dance the tango, Mary Pickford, Douglas Fairbanks senior and junior, Paul Whiteman, Ruby Keeler, who later married Al Jolson, Al Capone, Sophie Tucker, Bing Crosby, Will Rogers, Jack Benny, Eddie Cantor, Bebe Daniels . . . the names are endless . . . Jack Dempsey in his bar, Louis Armstrong, Duke Ellington, Marie Dressler, Irving Berlin – 'He was a good song writer,' Roy said, 'but he wouldn't have made a good crooner.' Someone came up to Roy and said, 'You play the trumpet very beautifully – just like a whisper.' It was Heifitz, and *Whispering* became Roy's signature tune. He got to know Darryl Zanuck well and they were often out together. The Warner Brothers were also his friends – Sam Warner, who launched the talkies, died twenty-four hours before *The Jazz Singer* made its first appearance on the screen.

Among the many girls who came from all parts of America in quest of film work was one with whom Roy fell in love. She had come from Chicago and her name was Harlean Carpenter. She was not pleased with that name and Roy selected 'Jean Harlow'. They were together for more than a year before a cable from London invited Roy: 'Can you open with band Cafe de Paris London September. Eight week engagement . . . wire confirmation.' He was distressed at having to leave Jean Harlow, but it was only a short engagement; after eight weeks he would be back. But the Cafe de Paris and London kept him much longer than he had expected: Jean Harlow got married and died young and Roy has spent the best part of forty years in England and is still here.

On his first evening at the Cafe de Paris Roy was approached by a young man who asked him to play *Without a Song* on his cornet. Roy wondered who it was and was told it was the Prince of Wales, who came nearly every night. Some years later in his hotel in Budapest Roy met the Prince of Wales, by then King Edward VIII, and Mrs Wallis Warfield Simpson, whom the King later married.

Roy's rise in fame and fortune was considerable. He had a beautiful house on Hampstead Heath, bought his first Rolls-Royce, travelled in various parts of the country with his band, attended Command Performances in England and Belgium, spent some months in Australia. When war broke out in 1939, because he had an American passport, Roy was unable to return to England and had to go back to America, where he met Danny Kaye at La Martinique where Roy had his band, and a young singer who made his first appearance in cabaret. 'You are probably the lousiest conductor I've had the misfortune of meeting,' the young singer said. Roy went to his dressing-room and really told him off. The singer's name was Frank Sinatra and Roy and he are now very good friends.

The book is packed with anecdotes, some sad, many fascinating and very amusing. It will give you happy hours of entertainment.

R J Minney.

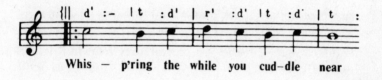

Whis — p'ring the while you cud-dle near

1. California Youth

BOY, OH BOY! What a journey!!

Little did I think when my mother and father brought my sister Vera and me to this place I'd feel so 'knocked out' . . . and am I tired. Funny little place . . . not many houses around. Vera who is seven can read a bit and I just heard her tell Mama the sign board over there says 'Hollywood'. Gee . . . I wish someone would give me a drink . . . you can get pretty thirsty on a trip like that, especially when that great big golden ball up in the sky makes you so hot. If I could walk I would get it myself . . . but I guess it is asking a lot for a guy who is only six months old to get around the way he'd like to.

This horseless carriage my mother pushes me around in could be a little more comfortable, but I guess you can't have everything. But mark my words . . . one of these days I'll get me one of those things people are riding around in, only both my horses will be white.

How could I possibly realize at such an early age just how many times that beautiful warm California sunshine would shine down on me, each and every summer on the beach at Santa Monica, making me resemble a Mexican who had been living in the Arizona desert. I'm sure I kept the vinegar industry alive by the amount of their product I consumed rubbing my body to keep from blistering – generally with little effect.

Well, I guess I'd better try and like this place because it looks as though we are going to stay a while so that my mother and dad can help all those unfortunate sinners be better people. That is why my mother is wearing that lovely bonnet with the ribbons tied under her chin. And my father's uniform lets everyone know they are both in the Salvation Army. I think they were sent out here from Denver, Colorado, to make California a better place. Well, if anyone can do the trick, they can. Especially my mother. No doubt about it . . . when everybody sees how beautiful she is they will want to be nice good people just to please her.

Thank goodness it hasn't taken long to find this little house where we are living. It's right in the middle of Los Angeles. We didn't stay in Hollywood because Mama and Papa said it was too far from Los Angeles where they would be stationed. We had to be nearer the mission in which they would be carrying on their work. That's a pretty big tree out there in the backyard – I'll be glad when I'm old enough to go out there and get onto that swing like Vera does with some of the other kids who are our neighbours . . .

I didn't know time could pass so quickly. Here I am celebrating my third birthday and my mother can bake a birthday cake better than anyone in the world and it's a good thing I have a lot of breath – I blew all three candles out at one go. Tonight Mama told me that now I was getting to be such a big boy she would take me to the 'street meeting' where the Salvation Army stand on a street corner and sing and play to all the people who gather around and then they tell everyone all about God and everything.

My mother and father can sing quite well and so can my sister. I will too when I get the chance. I know the words already because I've heard them so many times at home. Well – here we are standing by the curb and all the traffic going by makes plenty of noise – I hope one of those horses won't run over us. Yes, it's a lot of fun singing some of these songs I know. And what do you think? The head man who is called 'Captain' has just asked me if I would like to sing a song all by myself . . .

After much consideration I agreed and he asked the drummer in the brass band to put his big bass drum down on the street so that I could stand on it while I made my debut. I selected a song which I thought would be most suitable for my voice called *When The Roll Is Called Up Yonder* and then the band played my introduction. Although my knees were knocking quite a bit I did manage to remember all the words. When I was singing some of the people threw money on the drum and then I knew I had 'arrived'.

I did this on several occasions and *When The Roll Is Called Up Yonder* became the number one song in my repertoire and I was very successful when it came to collecting money in this manner. My mother was also very good when she went into saloons among all those tough characters with her tambourine. They would take one look at her, then without hesitation would empty their pockets. She never had any difficulty in those places as the 'Army' was very highly respected for the wonderful work they did for the 'down and outs'. Anyone could have free food and lodging for the asking. Of course Christmas and Thanksgiving Day always brought smiles to the faces of many who had almost forgotten what a 'square meal' had tasted like – and although I was rather young at the time I can still remember the happiness a 'new' suit and a bath would bring to those in such need.

I still don't know why, but my family decided to leave the Salvation Army and my father became a carpenter and painter. He was very handy with tools and you could see quite a lot of signs he had painted around Los Angeles in front of shops and on their windows. I was quite proud whenever I saw one, but unfortunately he wasn't all that successful in his work so my mother started to work for a friend of ours who owned a bakery shop near where we lived. Now my mother had a way with pies and, starting at about five each morning, she would turn out the most delicious ones and trade really began to boom. As I myself had reached the ripe old age of seven I thought it about time I should do my bit to help build up the family fortune and I decided to go into the newspaper business. Every evening after school you could find me on the street corner near my mother's bakery, selling papers. I never was very good with money and therefore my sister Vera would act as accountant – helping me give change when it was a little too much for me due to my lack of experience in the world of high finance. This was prompted by my giving one man change for a large coin he handed me, that more than took all the profit I had accumulated that day, plus a little more besides. But to off-set this I considered I was doing the public a good service by keeping them well informed on world affairs, like who won the Jess Willard-Jack Johnson World Title Fight, or the all-important baseball scores. Then there were the 'extras', telling all about the great disasters. It was very exciting knowing I was holding in my hand some of the most incredible news one could wish to read – and it was theirs for only one cent!

This gave me a feeling of importance and I realized the need to branch out. Yes, I thought I had better get one of those corners where more people were passing by – maybe near the streetcar station. Here I ran into my first snag! The guy who had sold the papers there for years didn't seem to need any help and inasmuch as he was older and bigger than I was, I didn't care to argue the point. So I continued going round our neighbourhood shouting the headlines, finishing off each startling announcement by crying: 'Read all about it'.

One day Mama decided that as we had quite a large backyard there would be plenty of room for some chickens, which not only would be a source of supply of good fresh eggs but sometimes a nice fat hen could be our Sunday afternoon meal – we always had our big dinner on Sunday afternoons. So Papa built a pen and soon we had all the eggs we wanted and the Sunday 'banquet' was a real treat. Luckily Vera liked the dark meat and I preferred white, so there was no problem in that direction. Then one day Vera and I talked our way into getting a bantam rooster and hen and it was our job to take care of them personally. When we fed the other chickens we sometimes gave ours a little extra! But the strangest thing happened every time Papa went into the pen. The bantam rooster flew up at at him and tried to peck him. He just didn't like my father and he wasn't long in showing it. After a while my dad got a little fed up with this caper and Vera and I watched him go into the pen with a broomstick in his hand and the moment 'banty' flew at him to peck him he smacked it on the head and it dropped to the ground and we knew our beautiful rooster had been slain! Papa, who was real mad, said, 'That will teach it a lesson'. Just as Vera and I had choosen a nice quiet place of burial it hopped up and shook itself and then ran around the pen as though nothing had happened. I guess he realized my father was bigger so he never tried that again.

There was one thing I used to like to do on a hot summer day. Just a few blocks away there was a factory where we kids used to go all the time. When we got there we would go inside into a large room. There in the corner was a great big barrel with a glass beside it and we could have a drink of this new *'thirst-quencher'*. It was free and we could have all we wanted. It tasted funny at first but it was cold and that was what was needed on those days when it was about eighty in the shade. Besides, a guy couldn't be too choosy when something was free even if it did have a peculiar name like Coca Cola.

Jasper was just about my number one 'bosom pal' by now. 'Jasper' – a kinda cockeyed name for a guy I thought. Boy, I'm glad my mother didn't call me that. But I liked him just the same, especially when he was my main source of information. Wasn't it Jasper who let me in on the highly confidential news about where we could get all that new drink we wanted, free of charge? Wasn't it Jasper who also told me about the place he had discovered where we could watch pictures that actually 'moved'? This I couldn't believe – but the Coca Cola was all he said it was and his first hand information had never let us down so far, so thinking he really must be 'kidding' this time, I said I would go with him, just in case by any chance he was telling the truth. We both went up to Main Street even though I knew very well that was exactly a place I shouldn't be in (I learned this from my mother) but the temptation was just too much. We stopped in front of a funny looking building and saw some pictures out in front of strange looking people with a lot of black marks around their eyes and the ladies with beautiful dresses on. There was a great big sign with 'Nickelodeon' on it and the sound of music was coming out through the front door. Then Jasper told me to look through the open door, where the curtain had been pulled aside, so that they could get some fresh air inside I guessed. Well – I couldn't believe my eyes! I just could not believe my own eyes! ! There on a big white curtain at the end of the room were some cowboys and Indians chasing each other on horses! They were actually running around that white sheet and people were sitting on chairs watching them. The exciting music was being played on a piano which didn't have anyone playing it. I later found out it was called a 'player' piano and it had a roll of paper that kept turning round and round with little holes in it. And boy, was it loud! Pretty soon a man came out and chased us away and told us not to come back. But little did he know Jasper and me. As soon as he went back again inside we feasted our eyes on something which just couldn't possibly be. Pictures that flickered and moved – I guess that was why they started calling them 'flicks' and 'movies'.

I just had to tell my mother and dad about this. I was sure Vera wouldn't believe me when I told her. But how was I going to let them know about this wonder without getting my backside spanked? I had promised my mother I wouldn't go 'up-town' without her or my father or Vera. But I was so excited I just had to take the chance, hoping they would be so overcome with this bit of information they would forget about the spanking. My luck was in owing to the fact that Mama was so happy to see me she hugged me very hard although she explained my supper was nearly spoiled by my staying out so late. And she had been terribly worried. But when I described what I had seen and the wonderment of it all I'm sure she forgot to tell Jasper how naughty she thought he was for keeping me out so late. She even asked him to stay for supper because she said there was plenty for both of us and she had kept it hot.

While we were eating Mama and Vera wanted to know everything we had done and seen and when my Dad came home from work (he was late too) both Jasper and I told him all about Billy The Kid and Sitting Bull who we saw chasing each other around on horseback, shooting with guns and bows and arrows at one another together with a lot of other cowboys and Indians. It was difficult to tell him how this all happened on a big white sheet! Hanging on the wall!

My mother and father decided then and there that the only way to find out what this was really all about was for all of us to go next Saturday night to see for ourselves – with the other people inside sitting on the chairs. I asked Papa if Jasper could come too and he said he thought he could manage it all right.

I never knew it could be so long until Saturday night, but it came at last and when Jasper came over about an hour early I had never seen him look so spic and span. His ears were still red where his mother had been scrubbing them so hard. And was I happy when we got on our way. I can still remember how thrilled Vera was. She kept asking me if the pictures really moved. The big moment came when my father went to the place where they sold the tickets (it cost each of us a nickel to get in) and when I saw them safely in his hand my heart bumped like that bass drum the man used to beat in the Salvation Army.

We were very lucky because we were nearly the first people in the line who were waiting to get in for the next show. And when we got inside we went right down in front of all the seats so we could see real good. In just a few minutes the whole place was full of people and it was very hot in there. We sat for a while and just as I was wondering when it would start the lights went out all at once. Then before I knew it they shone a sign on the big sheet and it said LADIES PLEASE REMOVE YOUR HATS. My mother said her hair didn't look very good but she did take her hat off and then that sign went off and another one shone on the sheet saying NO SMOKING. I'll bet my father was glad he didn't smoke. I asked Vera why she was smiling and she said she wasn't going to take her hat off because she wasn't wearing one.

Mama sat between Jasper and me and the next thing that happened was that the piano began to play real loud and then all of a sudden there was some flickering on the white curtain and some writing which told the name of the movie. Then some more flickering and we saw a movie all about a great train robbery. The train robbers hit the telegraph operator on the head and knocked him unconscious and when the train stopped the robbers took out their guns and held up the train. Then the picture stopped and the white sheet just had a bright light shining on it. Then another sign said JUST A MOMENT PLEASE WHILE THE OPERA-TOR CHANGES A REEL. Then a sign said ALL PERSONS ARRIVING LATE MAY REMAIN FOR THE NEXT SHOW.

Jasper and I were having a little trouble reading the lines of writing they had on the sheet while the picture was showing so Mama read them out to us – especially the long ones. Then the picture came back again after we were told by the writing what was happening. After the robbers had held up the train they all went into a saloon and got very drunk and were real mean. Mama told Jasper and me that that was what happened to you when you drank whisky. I got real scared when the picture was just about all over – one of the robbers came right up close and took out his revolver and pointed it right at me and pulled the trigger! It's a good thing it was only a 'flick'. I didn't make much headway when I asked my father if we could possibly stay and see it again but he said it was much too late and anyway Mama said we hadn't been late arriving so it would be dishonest to stay any longer.

When we got home and I went to bed I did not sleep very well because I kept thinking about those robbers and especially about the one who shot right at me at the end. Papa came home one night and said a friend of his had told him about another kind of moving picture show he had been to that really should be seen. And the very next Saturday night Papa took all of us up-town to a place where a big crowd of people were standing out in front, trying to get in. We had to wait in a long line with a lot of others and at last we moved up to where a man dressed like a conductor on a train was selling tickets and another man dressed the same way showed us to our seats. But instead of chairs the seats were just like the ones I'd noticed on the train coming to California from Denver and the whole thing looked exactly like a railway carriage. I didn't quite understand why it looked like that but pretty soon an engine bell started to ring very loud and the carriage began to rock back and forth just like being on the train again. Then the lights got dim and at the end of the car the curtains opened and there was another big white sheet.

As we watched it we could see the rails in front of us and we were moving very fast along the track watching the scenery go by. I think I felt a little sick but I was too excited to pay much notice. The bell kept clanging and everyone had a lot of fun seeing all those mounains and rivers and everything. Once or twice the picture stopped because the man in the uniform got up and said the film had broken and had to be fixed. While this was being done some man came in with a tray of popcorn and anyone who wanted to could buy it. He kept saying in a very loud voice: 'Get your hot buttered popcorn'. Funny, I didn't feel like eating popcorn for the very first time in my life, because I was 'train-sick' and it was kind of hot in there. Before long, as soon as the film was fixed, we'd be on our way again with more beautiful scenery. But right then and there I decided I liked cowboys and Indians better. I always liked the hero and I wished I could be like him and ride a horse the way he could – boy, I'd get me a few Indians! This time when it was over and we went outside I looked at the electric sign and it said HALE'S TOURS. The man at the door told Papa these train movie shows were in all the large cities – they had started 'back east'. But me, I preferred seeing people acting, rather than just the scenery.

All this time my mother was still working at the bakery and taking care of Vera and me. She practically worked day and night and I'm sure no two children ever went to school looking any cleaner than we did. But on our way home from school sometimes we would hear the fire engine racing down the street and as it would pass us belching great sparks and smoke, Vera and I would run along after it. I have never seen horses gallop so fast! And when we got to the fire we saw the firemen climb up the ladders and squirt water onto the flames from a long hose. They were really brave men to do that and some of them carried axes. Their hats were sort of strange looking and if it was summer time Vera and I would take off our shoes and stockings and wade in the water which was running down the gutter. It made our feet nice and cool but Mama wasn't very glad to see us both looking like we did when we arrived home. She asked why we didn't try to keep nice and clean so she wouldn't have to do so much washing. Vera and I were always sorry – until we saw the next fire engine!

Although I came from a home where any form of sin was looked upon with a certain amount of disfavour, I must admit that for a short spell I did manage to do a bit of swearing! Mostly while walking along the sidewalks looking for cigarette cards which had been disposed of by smokers along with the empty package. My fellow traveller on these occasions was my friend Jasper and our entire conversation consisted of the most filthy words little boys could think of. We generally shouted to one another while *en route* to the next portrait of Babe Ruth or some other famous baseball player whose face was printed on the card along with their biography. The great thing was to collect a series of your favourite sports personalities. I remember more than once some nice little old lady looking at my pal and me naturally thinking what naughty boys we were and sometimes telling us so. But this had little effect on me.

One night my father returned from work and asked me to accompany him into the bedroom where he explained that quite by accident he had been up on his ladder painting a sign on a window in the front of a shop when he was rather surprised to hear his son giving forth with some of the most vile language he had had the misfortune of hearing. He told me he wasn't going to spank me but he was sure I realized how wrong it was to talk like that and he would leave it to my better judgment as to whether I wanted to disgrace myself and my family in that manner. He left me in the bedroom to think it over and I still do not know to this day if it was that I saw the error of my ways or the sound of the fire engine coming down the street at breakneck speed which helped me to make up my mind so hurriedly to try to lead a better life. Upon receiving my father's blessing for my decision, in a wink I had already caught up with the fire engine and this caused me to wonder just what my mother would say when she saw the hole burned in the arm of my shirt where a spark from the smoke stack had alighted. The fire was very disappointing because the firemen put it out before I had a good chance to settle down to watch it. But anyway I wanted to get home to count the cigarette cards I had gathered that day. Those very cigarette cards started me on the road to another little thing my parents were not the least bit happy about – gambling! You see, when in the school yard during recess, a bunch of guys would get together and whip out their cards and play a game called 'matching'. Your 'foe' would be anyone who would like to throw a card on the ground by spinning it and then you would try to match it by spinning your card onto the ground and if his card was face up and yours landed face up you would win. If not the cards were his. This I considered was quite a good way of collecting the best and largest series in the entire school. So I tried it for the first time one recess and to my amazement I went home without a single one of those hard earned beautifully coloured cards of baseball players which I had intended to stick on my wall near my bed that very night. But I'd show them! After scouring every sidewalk for miles around I soon accumulated another 'stake' and I guess I never have been any more excited when entering any casino in the South of France than I was to get back in that school yard to take on again that guy who had relieved me of my highly prized possessions.

One night at supper time Mama called Vera and me into the house just after I had fed the chickens and while we were eating she told us she and Papa had decided to buy a candy store of our own. She said they had saved enough money after paying all expenses like rent, food and clothing to get a place they had looked at on Fifth street in Los Angeles. Boy oh boy, was I hearing right? A candy store! Imagine anybody saving enough money to buy a candy store!

Mr Tobey, the man who owned the bakery, was awfully sorry to have Mama leave because her pies were so outstanding, and anyway I liked Mr Tobey. He had given me a pair of gauntlet gloves with a red star on the side of them when I had done well in my lessons. But after waiting for what I thought was much too long, the candy store was ready to open. As soon as we got started my father, who was a sort of jack-of-all-trades, not only made home-made candy but also candied popcorn which I found on close inspection to be very tasty. The popcorn was wrapped in paper wrappers and we sold it at different parks where I liked to take it for delivery as it gave me the opportunity to get into a canoe and play like an Indian paddling around the lake just like they did in the movies. On more than one occasion I had to explain when I arrived home why I'd had to borrow the twenty-five cents for the hire of the canoe – but my mother nearly always understood just how important the exercise was for my muscles! Maybe that was one of the reasons I remained so skinny and all the kids called me 'Skeeter'.

After school and on Saturdays and Sundays I would help sometimes behind the counter selling candy and much to my great joy we had a soda fountain. I just couldn't wait to become the 'soda-jerk' because it hadn't been that often I had the wherewithal to satisfy my taste for nearly as much as I wanted of that wonderful delicacy – ice-cream! But now here I was with the magic power to prepare any kind of delicious creation anyone could wish for. Where to start first? Would it be an ice-cream soda? A malted milk? A milk shake or a frosted orange? Then of course it might be a pineapple sundae? How could a guy make up his mind when such an important decision was at hand? By vote naturally! Decided by a committee of one. It wasn't lunch time yet so I had plenty of room, and nothing to interfere. Yes – no doubt about it – that malted milk was going to be hard to beat! It was probably the best one I had ever tasted – I guess maybe because I had put a little extra malted milk into it. Now for the ice-cream soda. The 'malted' was chocolate so maybe strawberry would be a nice change? This was good too, but no hurry! There was still the raspberry milk shake to come and it was topped off by the frosted orange. That extra scoop of ice-cream made that one a little rich, but I still had just about enough room for the last entrant in this great ice-cream competition – the pineapple sundae! There, that was made and to do it full justice just a few chopped walnuts! By this time my tongue could have been used for a ski run. But first this delectable frozen morsel. Now for the grand finale! Which one was going to be my favourite of favourites? I started to review the situation and the more I reviewed it the less I liked thinking about it and as the doctor was leaving I heard him tell Mama not to let me have any more ice-cream for a day or two.

To make both ends meet we all lived in the rear of the store which was partitioned off from the front and this saved a great deal in rent which was so important for survival in those days. This was a little hard getting used to after living in the house we had rented for so long, but my mother said if we all worked hard and saved our money, some day we would have a house of our own again. She of course was the practical one in our family and now I realize just what a wonderful family we were. Good, honest, hard working people and that I suppose is the reason I never drank or smoked. Drink, cards and cigarettes were not allowed in our house but I must admit that once I did have a go at smoking. I used to sneak away from prying eyes and roll my own. They consisted of the finest choice dried leaves I could find, rolled in the more expensive Sunday newspaper, but although I tried my best to emulate the big guys, I found I had to 'swear off' at the age of five, never to smoke another cigarette. Drink never bothered me as I didn't like the taste of anything I had the odd chance to try. I should say that was probably the luckiest thing that ever happened to me as I was to spend so much of my life in night clubs.

But it did affect someone whom I learned to like as a friend. It was a man who used to come into our store and he was always alone and sometimes a little the worse for wear. He and liquor didn't seem to get along very well together. He was such a nice person and my mother and father befriended him, so when he was lonely he would come in and have a soda just to pass the time. I'm sure he would have much preferred a good stiff shot of whisky but he generally tried to be on his best behaviour when he came in. He would bring Vera and me toys or little things we would like. Then one day I was running down the street near the shop and I saw a crowd gathered around some person lying on the sidewalk and when I went over to see what they were looking at I saw there my good friend who had just blown his brains out! That is a thought I have never been able to erase from my memory.

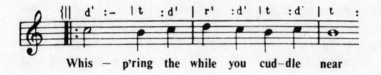

Whis — p'ring the while you cud-dle near

2. My 'Royal' Cornet

WELL IT HAPPENED one day! Yes, the day which really was the starting point of my life as it is today. There I was standing looking in the window of a second-hand store near our place and I saw the shiniest nickle plated cornet I'd ever seen. I'd seen many things in many windows of second-hand stores but somehow this was different. That cornet seemed to be asking me to come in and take it home with me – and its black leather case was just beside it. Strange I had never noticed a horn like this before, but somehow this was something I just had to have, then maybe I could learn to play like Johnny who used to play in the Salvation Army Band. The only catch was, I didn't have the cash. I wondered if my mother would – no, she didn't have that much money. It cost eleven dollars, it said so on the little sign, and that was a lot! Especially for a guy who was only eleven years old. Should I ask Mama, I wondered?

That night I waited until I thought my mother was in a good mood, then I took advantage of the fact that I knew she loved me very much and I told her all about the only thing in all the world which would make my life complete. If she could possibly manage to buy it for me I would pay her back some day, I promised. She asked me if I had any idea just how much eleven dollars was and I told her I knew, but it was a bargain that shouldn't be passed up and I would be a good boy and work real hard to help her do anything she wanted me to do. She said she would have to think it over though she didn't believe there was much chance, but I knew that if it were at all possible she would do it some way or other.

When I came home from school the next day Mama took me up the street to the second-hand store 'just to look'. Yes, it was still there right in front of our very eyes. I explained again what a fine bargain it was and at last I got her into the shop to talk to the man. I had all my fingers crossed plus my toes and when she asked me if I was *really* sure I wanted it and would learn to play it, my heart nearly jumped right out of my body. The most important deal of my life was completed on the spot and never again could I expect to be as happy as I was at that moment. Yes, sir! That was when and how it all started!

I just couldn't wait to get my horn home so that I could give it a real good polish, even though its gleaming brightness was already a sight to behold. But a little silver polish might make it all the more dazzling. Gee whiz! I wondered if I could blow it! In just a few more steps we would see. I wished Mama would walk faster. Papa and Vera were awaiting the outcome of our trip to the store and when they saw me carrying the beautiful leather case my sister threw her arms around me and nearly knocked me down. In about two seconds I was showing not only my father and sister the most terrific horn a boy could possess but also the customers who happened to be in our shop, and it was agreed by all that that cornet was undoubtedly a thing of beauty.

After sparing them more time than I had intended, the next item on the agenda was, how to blow it? I knew I had the breath, after all I had never failed to blow out every candle on my birthday cakes with only one great big blow, so I was sure I was all right in that department. And when I ran home from school I wasn't out of breath like some of the kids. Now to give it a try! I put the mouthpiece in the horn and put it to my lips, and believe me that old wolf didn't have a thing on me when he threatened to 'huff and puff and blow the house down!' I nearly shattered the windows with my very first blast which turned out to be one of the most peculiar noises I had yet heard. I knew at once that I didn't quite have the hang of it. So I tried again and again and then I knew for sure I was doing something wrong. It couldn't possibly be my wind because I blew that cornet louder than any I had ever heard. But what came out of it was the disturbing part of the whole exercise.

Vera even tried to help me by blowing it and she experienced quite some difficulty when instead of putting the mouthpiece to her lips and blowing, she put it inside her mouth and even I knew she was trying to do it the hard way. My mother finally came up with the only sensible suggestion. Why didn't I wait until tomorrow, then go down the street after school to see Mr Showalter, the old German shoemaker. He had a little shop and Mama said she had heard him playing a cornet some nights after he had closed. This was music to my ears. I'm sure I didn't learn a great deal in class the next day, and the moment school was out I dashed off with the speed of a guy who was going to surprise the world with his prowess on the most beautiful cornet in the entire universe and Mr Showalter was going to be the magician to help me perform this miracle. I was still puffing when I reached his shop and when I told him what I had in mind, his face lit up with a smile and he said that not only would he show me how to blow the instrument, but he would also teach me the scales and how to press the right valves at the right time. I knew at that very moment the only reason I was put on this earth was to become the best cornetist anyone had ever heard. But of course there were a lot of notes to be blown before I set the world on fire.

Mr Showalter closed shop early that evening because I'm sure he had an ulterior motive. I found out later that he had always wanted someone to play duets on the cornet with him. When he saw my shiny horn he was taken aback more than a little because his old standby cornet was showing the wear and tear he had given it and he must have wondered how a boy of eleven could be the possessor of an instrument of such quality. He said that after he had shown me how to blow it he would like to play a tune on it, but I was more interested in getting down to business so that I could amaze people with my dexterity.

Well, I thought he was slightly off his rocker when he asked me to show him what I would do if I had a thread on my tongue. This took a fair amount of considering because I didn't remember having a thread on my tongue for quite some considerable time and I had forgotten just how I got rid of it. He said he supposed I would spit it out like most people would who discovered they had a thread on their tongue, and I thought the wise thing would be to agree. He even showed me how he would do it and asked me to follow suit. I felt kind of silly because I didn't have anything on my tongue to spit out, but Mr Showalter praised the way I spat and then he asked me to put the mouthpiece of my cornet up to my lips and press it *lightly* against my lips and spit out the thread on my tongue. This made me wonder if a shoemaker really knew how to teach a boy how to blow a cornet. But to please him I did it just the way he said and *presto!* the most beautiful sound I or anyone else ever played on a horn came out of the end of it. A magician indeed – this was Merlin at his best and I wondered how many beautiful notes my mother could have played every time I had seen her spit a thread off her tongue while sewing. He asked me to do it again but that time it wasn't quite so extraordinary. So he made me try over and over again until I was pretty sure I wouldn't make one of those peculiar sounds which were rather frightening. I don't remember spitting so much as I did that first hour, but the notes got better and better and once or twice they sounded almost sweet.

The days passed and Mr Showalter kept to his word. He showed me how to play the different scales and how to finger the valves as he had promised, and when I went home my sister Vera would help me memorize what he had taught me. You see, that was really the extent of my musical education as a cornet player. I never did take private lessons and soon this old shoemaker and I would sit out in his back yard behind his shop every chance we had and we started to play easy duets. It was a wonderful place to play, there under the bright sun, out in the air, and I recall that some of the neighbours weren't too happy about the whole idea, but most of them didn't seem to mind it. I guess they were my very first audience as a cornet player. One thing which I remember, Mr Showalter had a very droopy moustache and after a while he had to do a mopping up job as the steam would accumulate on it after a long blow. But he was very kind to me and I owe him more than I can say.

After giving duet 'concerts' in the back yard for a time, our tone quality must have altered considerably judging by the improvement in our 'foreign relations' with the neighbours as exemplified by the warm reception we would receive on occasion, especially when we were both in tune at the same time. And I was beginning to be able to read the notes much faster, greatly helped of course by the fact that music was the only subject in school at which I could be described as gaining something relatively close to good marks. It transpired I could read notes better than the written word and this made Mr Showalter beam with joy when he realized he was such a good teacher. Sometimes he would get so wrapped up in his work he would blow so hard his droopy moustache would stick out like a hair brush and when he came quite by accident to a pretty note he was in complete ecstasy and would keep it going far too long just so he could listen to it.

As Vera had developed a very beautiful soprano voice and, not to be outdone, was learning to play the saxophone, it wasn't long before we were playing duets together. She was very musical and later added the piano to her accomplishments and she would accompany me while we played our favourtie pieces. I guess there never was a better audience than Mama. The wonderful encouragement she gave me brought me on so quickly that my playing improved at a fast rate. We used to have a machine that played records and the music came out of a beautifully coloured horn and I used to join in with my cornet with some of the pieces I knew. Having a natural ear for music, I was one of those lucky people who didn't have to 'knock their brains out' to learn to play, and now that I look back I am positive it would have been much better in every way if I'd had to apply myself to what music was really all about. It would have been most helpful all along the way. This may sound strange coming from a person who has attained what is known as success in many countries of the world, but in those days things came much more easily. Being a master-craftsman on your instrument with a fine musical background was not nearly so important as it is today.

Not being one to overdo the practice bit I just allowed the horn practically to play itself. Most of the kids I knew had to spend hour after hour trying to master the violin or piano, but once I got started it all came easy, too easy.

One day when I took enough time off from playing baseball with the kids to allow my mother to have a word with me, she told me she and Papa were selling the candy shop and moving out to a place called Belvedere just near Los Angeles. There was a nice house they were going to buy and it would be our own and they were also purchasing a small restaurant. I didn't like the idea of leaving my friends but the thought of having our own house with my own bedroom instead of living in the rear of the candy store was very exciting. I supposed I would miss all those ice-cream sodas and candy and popcorn and everything, but I guessed it was for the best, which it was. The house was nice and my father, being a pretty good carpenter among other things, soon had it looking very well. He added some bookcases and things to make it all the better and then there was a lovely green lawn in front and a large yard in the rear so that we could have a garden. Mama soon bought some chickens, and having our own home-grown vegetables and fresh eggs and Sunday chicken was something we all enjoyed and the flowers we planted made the place look very pretty.

Our newly acquired restaurant consisted of a counter

where food was served and there were about four tables.
Then my father built along the front window what was
known as a 'steam table', a sort of galvanized iron tank
which held hot steaming water with large holes in the
top of it where pans of food were placed to keep hot.
This became quite popular with the people who wanted
to buy home-made food to take away with them, as
both my mother and father were good cooks. Before
long we had a good steady trade and I did my stuff as
waiter in the evenings after school, which was quite
nearby.

All this time my playing was improving and I was
asked by a man and his wife who had a small orchestra
if I would like to play with them. I explained to them
I had never played in public before but they said that
it was only for a bit of pleasure. This sounded all right,
so once a week we would all meet in the parlour of their
small house and play some music I was just about able
to handle. That's when I first learned I had a most
frightening inferiority complex. I was so scared each
time it came to my turn to play I got a *vibrato*
resembling the kind a nanny-goat gives out. Strangely
enough that terrible feeling remained with me practically all through my professional career. Even when I
was on stage at the world famous Palace Theatre in
New York City, or at the Palladium in London, I was
always nervous. But back in that little house, on my
very first introduction to the orchestral world,
butterflies nearly spoiled this wonderful chance that was
given me. However, I did manage to get through the
evening all right and I was very pleased when the man
and his wife asked me if I would come along again at
the next get-together. I can admit now, I was quite
proud of myself.

This led to the wife, who played the piano in the

orchestra, asking me, after we had rehearsed together for a while, if I would like to play my cornet in a small movie house where she was engaged to give the movies atmosphere with her rendition of 'hurry' music when the train was about to run over the heroine who was tied to the track, or something to wring your heart out when the lovers were about to be parted. She said there would only be the two of us and it would be good experience for me. I was really thrilled at the prospect of being a cornetist in a place where I could see all the films I wanted to and it wouldn't cost me a penny. I could not wait to tell my mother the wonderful news but when she heard it she pointed out that the cinema was way on the other side of town, quite near Hollywood, and not only would it be much too late at night when I got home after working there, but it would be rather costly, keeping in mind there was no remuneration. But her main objection was that I would miss so much sleep on account of having to get up early in the morning for school.

Well, that was a real heartbreaker. To think my mother would do this to me, would actually stand in my way, when I had such a marvellous opportunity of being someone in the world of music. I didn't care about not getting any money. I just thought of being able to see 'Bronco Billy' and stars like John Bunny and Flora Finch every night of the week. My life was in ruins and just as I was trying to get over the sadness of it all an astounding thing happened. Right out of a clear blue sky the man who owned the Bijou Kinema near our house asked me if I would care to play my cornet just on weekends with the piano player who worked there. This was too much! To think I was in such demand – and Mama surely would have no objection now, and she didn't. I wouldn't have to work for nothing, I could have all the tickets for the shows I wanted and I wouldn't be losing any sleep. Well, well! I guess my mother knew a thing or two, for she had told me something else would happen for me if I'd just forget the other job on the other side of town, and sure enough this was it. My number one strong point was that every time the troops came on the scene and rescued the wagon train I would blow the loudest bugle any bugle boy could blow. In fact the owner of the Bijou told me on one occasion I was blowing everyone out of his Kinema! So I took it easy until the next time I got excited. But at the end of the week I was given tickets for all the family for the next week's show and I was mighty proud when I took Mama, Papa and Vera the following week to see Pearl White in one of her spine-chilling serials. It was always a long wait until the next week to find out if the buzz-saw was going to cut her in half.

During each screening of the film programme when I would walk up the aisle at intermission time I could feel everyone's eyes on me and I knew they were saying to themselves: 'There goes that boy who plays the cornet so well,' and I was beginning to feel rather important. I realized my playing enhanced the enjoyment of what was shown on the screen because you must understand that, aside from all those bugle calls, I joined in with the pianist every time I knew the piece she was playing and I'm sure the feeling I put into my playing during a sad scene helped to bring tears to many an eye. I even noticed a certain mark of respect at school from my fellow class-mates. I was truly thankful for the day I first saw that beautiful horn in the window. By the way, I think I forgot to mention the name of my cornet. It was a 'Royal'. No wonder I liked it. It had the name Roy on it!

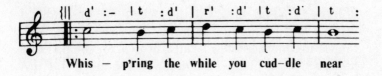

Whis — p'ring the while you cud–dle near

3. The Next Step

THE NEXT STEP along the road to success happened when I met a boy who was a very good saxophone player. His name was Ivan and he was about eighteen years old, and when he heard that I played the cornet he asked me if I would like to come to a rehearsal of a brass band of which he was a member. It was called The Los Angeles Examiner Newsboys' Band. That was a band sponsored by the newspaper bearing its name and it didn't take long for me to accept his offer for I thought it was about time I started to branch out a bit after my success at the Bijou.

When the conductor of the band heard me play he said he thought he could find a place for me in the band, and upon hearing these words I forgot my nervousness. I had as usual been so scared I was nearly sick. When I hurried home to tell my family I'm sure we were the happiest people for miles around. How proud they were of me. Then after much rehearsing the big night came at last – the night I was actually to become a member of this outstanding musical aggregation. Here I was, a boy of thirteen, playing alongside musicians who were mostly men, and when we started

43

marching down the streets of Los Angeles that night playing marches composed by John Philip Souza I was truly in heaven and all my dreams were coming true. I must explain though, that it was slightly difficult for me to keep my mouthpiece tight against my lips while marching, since I'd always sat down before. More than once I stumbled over the street-car tracks and this was added to the fact that I was wearing a uniform cap which had belonged to another musician (he must have had a much larger head than I had) and it kept slipping down over my eyes and ears. This, plus the inconvenience of the coat sleeves I had to turn up so that I could use my hands. I suppose I did look sort of funny in that rather too long coat, as I was still wearing short pants. The only kid in the band, but the older guys were very helpful and kept shouting encouragement.

We finally reached our destination which was right outside the Head Office of the *Examiner* on Broadway and we all formed a semi-circle at the curb while standing in the street. There was a large crowd of people waiting for us and sure enough, there was Mama, Papa and Vera, all beaming with expectation. I tried to look as though I had been doing this kind of thing all my life, but inside me – boy was I nervous! How I ever got through that first concert I will never know, but I came out of it unscathed and afterwards the conductor told me he was very pleased, and Ivan and the rest of the men said I was great. My mother showed her appreciation of my fine work by buying me the biggest ice-cream soda I had seen since I used to make them for myself.

This achievement added to my confidence greatly but not enough to stop the butterflies on each and every occasion the band appeared, sometimes at the Pasadena Orange Show and at other festivals, and often in large

parades on New Year's Day or the Fourth of July,
Independence Day. As a matter of fact I became quite
useful in the band, substituting for a drummer when he
was sick or maybe playing the 'peck-horn' (E-flat alto)
when that position needed to be filled. This I didn't
care much for as all I had to do was to play a most
uninteresting part, and I liked to play the 'lead' which
produced the melody.

At rehearsal one night the bandmaster said someone
from a movie studio had telephoned him to ask if he
had someone who could play bugle calls on a horn and
he told them he had the very boy for what they wanted.
He said the job was mine if I wanted it and when I
heard just what was required I couldn't say 'yes' quickly
enough.

The next day I had to go out all the way from my
house to Hollywood where the big studios of Famous
Players Lasky were on Sunset Boulevard at Vine Street.
I'd heard a lot about this place and I was thrilled to be
just near it. Very timidly I went to the outer office and
told the man in uniform sitting behind the desk that I
wanted to see Mr Cecil B De Mille. He kinda gave me
a funny look and asked if I had an appointment and I
said I thought so. He asked me what I wanted to see Mr
De Mille about and I thought this was a rather rude
question, prying into other people's business, but he
seemed a nice man so I thought I would tell him.

When he heard I was on a very special mission he
smiled and asked a little boy dressed in a bright
uniform to take me to my destination. I saw the boy
taking a good look at me and I bet he was wondering
how a boy of my age could get in to see the Great
Master himself. I thought I would keep him guessing,
no need to give all your secrets away to a stranger. I did
notice a note of respect in his attitude though.

After going through several doors and out into a yard where there were many large buildings we came to one where we went in through another door. When we got inside I saw the most beautiful great big room all made of glass with a great long staircase in the centre. The boy said it was a ballroom 'set'. I made out like I knew what he was talking about.

Everybody was very busy and there were a lot of glaring lights which made the glass shine. Gee whiz! What if it should all break. The man the little boy took me to said he'd wondered what had happened to me and seemed glad I was there. I thought that was nice, he didn't even know me. Well, he took me over to a great high stand built out of a lot of boards and we climbed up a long ladder and when we got to the top I nearly got dizzy, but as soon as he gave me a chair to sit in I began to watch all those different people running around working. I hadn't seen big cameras like those since Mama and I had seen them at Santa Monica when the Keystone Cops used to fall off the end of the pier into the water.

At that moment I saw a bald head appearing over the top of the platform I was sitting on. He had to climb the ladder too and he was a little bit out of breath. When he got up there the man that followed him up called him Mr De Mille and I knew I was looking at this great director I had heard so much about. When he spoke to the man I thought he sounded just like the actors I'd heard. Then he turned to me and sort of stared at me and I wondered when he was going to say something. At last he did, he said, 'Hello, boy.' I felt pretty good when he said this. I couldn't tell if he smiled a little bit, but after some thought he said: 'I assume you are going to assist me in getting *Quiet* on this set when need be.' Just think this great man speaking to me like I was of quite some importance. As soon as he asked me that, I said without any hesitation, 'Yes, sir.'

He seemed pleased at this and so I just sat there and waited until he said something else, but he didn't. I thought this was a bit unfriendly, but then I supposed he had something he was thinking about.

There was one of the biggest megaphones beside him I ever saw and when he felt like it he hollered 'SILENCE!' I thought everybody had fainted they were so still. Then he turned to me and said so everybody could hear him: 'Boy, when I touch you on the head I want you to give me a loud bugle call, good and loud, I *must* save my voice.' Oh boy, I wondered if Mr De Mille knew how loud I could blow my horn. Hadn't I almost blown them out of the Bijou? Maybe that was why the bandmaster had sent me for this special job. He realized my strength. So the first time Mr De Mille touched me on my head I let loose and everyone jumped. What a look of admiration Mr De Mille gave me. I felt very flattered. Then the very next time he touched me I really practically blew the end right off my horn and that time he said: 'Easy, boy, we don't want to wreck this glass set!' I learned by this remark that he knew how much power I had.

After nearly blowing myself silly the day drew to a close and Mr De Mille patted me, saying how much he appreciated how loud I could blow and hoped we would meet again. By this time I had fallen head over heels in love with Gloria Swanson!

Yes, Gloria Swanson! And at that very early age my natural instinct told me that she was a most beautiful lady. I had never seen anyone who looked like her before and when she walked down the huge glass staircase I forgot my bugle calls just long enough to notice she wasn't wearing very many clothes. I think that was the one moment when Mr De Mille had to tap me twice on the head before I awakened to the fact that I was holding up the entire production by being so enraptured by so lovely a vision. But being the professional I was I proceeded to blast everyone's ears off with my loudest bugle call yet. That's what a beautiful woman can do to a guy. Every time I wasn't blowing, my young eyes could never leave this famous star I had by this time seen in several films, and never had I dreamed that I would be sitting next to this great director bewitching his great star's every move while actually making a real movie.

About five years later I was to learn that this beautiful lady was one of the nicest people I was ever going to meet in the film business. Quiet and charming and not at all like some of the characters she portrayed on the screen. Very softly spoken – always dressed in the best of taste. But at this moment I rather liked that dress she was wearing in this picture although I was sure my mother would have been just a little perturbed had she known her favourite and only son was associating with people like that.

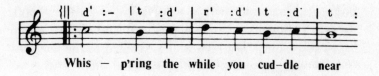

Whis — p'ring the while you cud-dle near

4. Girls

JUST ABOUT THIS time a rather disturbing thing was happening to me. I began to suspect that I was beginning to like girls! I was almost sure of it when one day at school I was conscious that that girl sitting across the class-room was quite pretty. *Hmmm* – (after taking inventory). Yes – prettier than the rest of the girls. I wonder how I had not noticed this before. No doubt about it, this girl was positively beautiful. At this point I vividly remember that Miss Carnahan, my teacher, asked me to get up before the class and read the essay we were all expected to write during the last half hour. Unfortunately, when casting my eyes in Letha's direction (yes Letha, that was her name) most of the allotted essay time had been spent considering her finer points, and when I admitted to Miss Carnahan I hadn't completed the essay, she helped me out on this point by allowing me all the time I needed to do so. That was after school, of course!

The next day during recess at lunch time I thought it might be a good idea if I were to explore the situation further in regard to Letha. She couldn't possibly be as

pretty as I had surmised in a weak moment. But there
she was sitting with two other girls, seemingly enjoying
her sandwiches when I casually strolled by to take a
closer look. Yes, this girl had just about everything the
pretty girls in the movies had. I still couldn't understand how I had missed this revelation in class, and
when I forgot my good manners and definitely stared at
her, she also brought her good upbringing into play by
smiling, which immediately put me into a state of
walking-on-air existence from that moment on.

That night when I said my usual prayers before going
to sleep, I added the name of Letha to the long list of
people I wanted God to take care of. I then knew that
I had at last found the only girl in the world for me.
Now I had to find some way of letting her know of my
high regard for her. This came along quite unexpectedly
when we were both asked to be in the school play. She
was going to be Snow White and I was given the role
of the Dwarf Leader. I had a song to sing, and as I sang
and was looking at Letha, the *timbre* of my voice
improved out of all recognition. Now I could appreciate
the way Romeo felt!

And this led me to getting up enough courage to ask
Letha if I could carry her books home from school and
she said they weren't heavy. But I mentioned the fact I
would be going that way anyway and might as well. So
my first real romance was under way the moment her
hand accidentally touched mine while handing over the
books. It even made me forget about my cornet for the
time being. Needless to say, I took her to parties such as
at Hallowe'en time when we used to duck for apples in
a barrel of water; and just to show her what an outstanding apple catcher I was, I nearly drowned myself.
But I did win the prize and I wonder if she still keeps
it?

At last – fourteen years old, and now that I was reaching 'manhood' it was essential I started looking the part. Again my mother was made the object of my newly-formed onslaught. The where-with-all to buy this requirement! Letha would certainly prefer going out with a guy who wore long pants, and a cornetist who was coming along in the world should be dressed in keeping with his position, so 'How about it, Mama?' She smiled at me and admitted she thought it about time I should make the kind of appearance I described to her.

My sister, Vera, was called upon to accompany me to Hollenbeck Park one Sunday afternoon so that I could try out my new suit. I do not think I would ever have gone by myself, but she gave me the courage I needed and, of course, I thought everybody was looking at me. But I soon got used to the idea and it wasn't long before I was playing in the brass band in that very park.

My friend, Ivan (who was becoming one of the leading saxophone players) was by this time playing in the band and he suggested that I should be in it. For the very first time I began to play for money! Not much of it, but it was only on Sundays and it gave me my own spending money. And, of course, Letha realized she was keeping company with a man of means who could on occasion buy her popcorn and a coke while boating on the lake between concerts. The boat was gratis for the boys in the band. I don't quite know if it was the sudden wealth or my new-found success but I started to wonder if I was becoming 'girl-crazy' because, although I had always been perfectly true to Letha, I found to my great surprise I had noticed another girl at school who was in the class ahead of me. This caused me a great deal of anguish as I knew I should not even dream of another girl but Letha. But this girl *was* kinda something, and although Letha's hair was golden this one had real black hair and blue eyes. No, I must put her out of my mind! And I did. . .

Then one day I saw her walking along the street with an older boy who had a pretty good reputation at school with the girls. For some unknown reason I felt a little jealous and I began to think here is a prize worth winning. But there was a little problem here. The guy was bigger than me and I had heard he was pretty handy with his fists and, being a person of a very friendly nature, I just didn't want to start any bad feelings. But I did rather fancy his girl! I heard she was quite a good tennis player and could often be seen on the tennis court at school. It was a good thing I had played a little tennis myself across the street from our house on a vacant lot with a net so full of holes you couldn't tell whether the ball went over it or through it. Any way, I could at least hit the ball, so the next day found me on the court at school and I discovered I could play a little better than I had thought. I did my best to look agile while playing as I noticed Frances would now and then look in my direction which was slightly off-putting and on one occasion I neatly put one of my hardest smashes squarely through the school window. This caused a bit of excitement and it gave me the chance of remarking to my quarry that I didn't realize I could hit a ball so hard. But she must have admired my strength because she suggested I become her doubles partner in the next match and, whereas I had been able at least to get the ball over the net most times, the mere fact that her lovely legs attracted my eyes more than the ball meant that I'm afraid I didn't do too well as a partner. But this did not seem to make so much difference to Frances. She said we must play together again sometime and I asked her if tomorrow was too soon. She agreed and that was the start of me being torn between two loves.

One day it would be Letha I loved, then it would be Frances, and during this time on outward appearances I was quite a ladies man, but inwardly I was more shy than a ladies man should be. Once when Letha and I were at the park and went on the Roller Coaster and we sat in the seat together, I ventured putting my arm around her and as she didn't slap my face I guessed she didn't mind. Then when the fast moving car was going round a curve my hand slipped and I felt something slightly protruding on her chest and neither of us said anything, but I realized one of the reasons girls are so attractive to boys.

Soon my problems were eased a bit as it was graduation time and I was about to leave grammar school and would be entering High School. The school chosen was the Polytechnic High School, very near the great big vacant property several blocks square where all the big circuses, like Ringling Brothers and Barnum and Bailey, always played.

Seeing this place took me back to the time when I was very small and Papa came home from work one evening and told us he had heard from a friend that the next day two men were going to be flying around in something called an aeroplane and as it should be very interesting he would take me to see them fly. He said it was going to be at the same place where they held the circus when it came to town. I asked him how they did it, but he said he didn't know himself. He had read something about it, but he had never seen one and really didn't know just how it was done. He only knew they had a kind of big machine that had some sort of wings and a motor that turned round and round, which made the machine fly through the air. Like a bird! This

I couldn't believe. But Papa said it was true and I thought he should know. But how could a thing like that possibly fly? Mama made me go to bed early so that I could get up early enough next morning to start on our way.

Well, here we are at the place where I had been to see the circus so many times, but now there weren't any tents. Just the great big vacant piece of land with so many people standing around that I don't think I have ever seen such a large crowd before in my life. Right down at the end of the field I can see some kind of a thing that everybody is crowding around and looking at, and there are plenty of policemen surrounding it – I guess so that people can't get too near. Papa says we can go down there and take a look if we can get close enough to it. I wish some of these people would get out of the way so I can see what's going on. There, that's better, sitting up here on Papa's shoulder, I'll bet I can see more than anyone else can. I had expected to see something like the kind of kites I make, but this isn't even the same shape. Sure enough, it has two wings, one above the other, and a part sticking out in the back – I just heard a man say he thought it was called the 'tail'. And in the front there is a thing that has two blades on it, each turned a little bit in different directions, and this is attached to a small motor. It's a funny looking contraption!

The two men inside the roped off space which the policemen are guarding and where the aeroplane is standing, are wearing caps and some kind of leggings. There are some other men with them and Papa says they are mechanics who help make the engine go. Papa told me the two men were the Wright Brothers – Wilbur Wright and his younger brother Orville: they built the very first heavier than air machine. Both are in their early thirties. I wish they would hurry and get started to fly in the air. Here is one of them now getting in the machine and sitting in the small seat near the motor in between the wings. Now a man is turning the 'propeller' (that's what the man next to me just called it). He is grabbing hold of it and trying to swing it around so that each time he does, it makes a loud noise as it starts to turn real fast. Boy, what a racket! Now it has stopped again and the smell of gasoline is getting up my nose. There, it's started!

The police are making all the people stand back. I'll bet they would all be knocked over if the police weren't there to get them out of the way. Now the propeller is turning round so fast that I have never heard anything like it, and the thing starts to move forward and the man in the seat is waving everyone aside as he glides along the ground at a very fast speed. Everyone is running after him and, all of a sudden, there it goes – off the ground! It is actually up in the air a little way and the people are yelling to the man in the seat. Then he starts to turn the aeroplane around in a kind of circle right over our heads and he is waving to us. This is something I'm sure I shall never forget, this great big flying machine going through the air quite high, with the man guiding it and all the people still screaming. The police are telling the people to stand back so that the man can come down again on to the ground.

Now there is a great big space in the middle of the field which is empty so that no one will get hurt when he comes down; and here he comes! – right down, toward where we are all standing around the empty space. The machine is gliding just like a bird does when it is landing and the wheels hit the ground pretty hard and the machine bounces a few times until it slows down and stops. And the big crowd all run over to where it is and Papa and I are just about the first ones there. But the police make us all stand back (there must be several hundred of us) and then the man hops out of the machine and his brother has come over to talk to him. I wish I could hear what they are saying. But they are both smiling and now the policemen are starting to tell us that is all there will be – the exhibition is over! Gee, I wish he would go up again! But Papa says we had better get out of the crowd and anyway, it is almost time for our lunch and Mama doesn't like to be kept waiting when she has cooked something for us. Later, on that very same land, I started running at athletic meetings after I had started at the Polytechnic. But first of all, there was the enrolment and my mother accompanied me on the day this took place. I was going to study to be an architect, which developed into a difficult thing to do as far as I was concerned. All those figures and algebra – everything that I wasn't too happy about. It was in fact a little more than I had bargained for. But soon I was asked to join the school orchestra and this made school a little more bearable. I also enjoyed being on the track team. At grammar school I had been the fastest kid, but when I competed against the older boys here I was less successful. Another added attraction was when some students showed me how to make wooden dice in our woodwork class, which sometimes proved to be so attractive I would forget about the importance of being in class and improving my studies. We would spend the time playing 'craps' in some out of the way place not too near the school. That was the reason I never did have any spending money!

Now I wasn't seeing quite so much of Letha and Frances, and I had met a fellow who was about three years older than me and he was a sharp dresser. He always had a nice suit on, with shirt and ties to match.

I wanted to be dressed like that, but it was impossible when you were going to school and didn't have much money. He was able to afford it because he was working at the Los Angeles Trust and Savings Bank. When I told my mother I would like to be able to work at that bank she let me know just how impossible it was. How could I even think of leaving school when it meant so much. She hadn't had much opportunity of having a good education, as her mother had died when she was eleven years old and she had regretted not being allowed to go to school when someone had to stay and take care of her smaller sisters and brothers. No, I could forget the whole thing! I did for a while, but architecture and I had nothing in common and I kept on at my mother until she decided she would probably not be seeing any of the buildings I had planned to build, and almost against her wishes I started at the Bank as messenger boy. The salary was twenty-five dollars a month, but that seemed quite a lot to me and anyway it wouldn't be long before I would take over as president of the bank. Then I would have much more money. And a boy of fifteen should have a lot of money. It was easy for me to keep my weight down while chasing from bank to bank and from department to department, and I did this for a while, when one day someone by the name of Ira Gay got in touch with me and asked me if I would like to play with his orchestra at the Los Angeles Country Club on Saturday nights. This Club was a well known Golf Course in Beverly Hills and the Saturday night dances were strictly class. It appealed to me, especially as I would be making more money. As it was I was able to give my mother some of my earnings but with this job I could give her much more.

It was just a small orchestra – piano, banjo, drums,

violin (which Ira played) and my cornet. After a few Saturday nights and the added money Ira paid me (which seemed like a fortune compared to the salary I was still getting at the bank), I began to notice that cornets were a little bit old fashioned. There was a new styled horn on the market called a trumpet and, of course, I had to have one. I went to a music shop and tried one out and at the very first blow it seemed much easier and the tone was much better. Better than my Royal! – the horn that had been my friend during all those days spent in the back yard with Mr Showalter playing duets; and didn't it help me blow all those exciting bugle calls at the Bijou? But best of friends sometimes have to part and this was one of those unhappy times. When I had to turn it over to the man in part payment for my new trumpet, it was a very sad moment. This new horn was silver and longer and very pretty, but it could never mean as much as my Royal had meant.

With the extra money each week I was now in a position to add to my wardrobe and not only did I get one or two new suits but I specially had some nifty silk shirts made to order. The vogue in natty wear for men was bright stripes that were very wide, with four inch wide tight cuffs with four buttons close together. The coat jackets were tight at the waist and flared at the bottom with bell-shaped sleeves. Trousers were also bell-shaped and the shoes were so pointed I nearly ruined my feet for life. But nothing was too uncomfortable if you were well dressed. And I was uncomfortable!

A few months later Ira Gay took me along with the orchestra to where we sometimes played at the Los Angeles Athletic Club in the heart of Los Angeles. This was in addition to the job we had at the Country Club and the money started to roll in. So not only was I working at the bank but on the two other jobs as well and my weekly earnings, which started with the free tickets I received at the Bijou, grew to something I hadn't dreamed of just a short time before.

It was about this time that my mother and father decide to separate, which came as a complete surprise to Vera and me. They sold the restaurant and the two of us lived with Mama in the house together. Then some little time later Vera married a fellow named Harvey. He was a really nice person and I was very glad for Vera. She rated a good guy as she had always been a wonderful sister to me. She and Harvey went to Bakersfield where he had a job with an oil concern. That left Mama on her own with me, and while I was away playing at night I knew she was very lonesome.

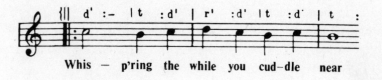

Whis — p'ring the while you cud-dle near

5. Bands and Clubs

BUT IN THE meantime a man approached me and said his son was getting a band together to play at Santa Monica and Ocean Park which were next door beach resorts, and they were going to play there for the summer season: the idea being that while his band was playing at one of the beaches a large military brass band would alternate with them while playing at the other. This man said he had heard my work and he would like me to join his son's band. There would be seven musicians in all. He offered me fifty dollars a week which was far in advance of what I was making on my three jobs. Then, if it could be arranged, my mother could have a good holiday by the seaside in the summer with me. She surely deserved it after all those years of hard work to help bring up Vera and me.

I went home and told Mama all about the offer and she didn't like the idea very much of my giving up my good steady position at the bank. But, as usual after much persuasion, she finally capitulated and I accepted the job. In any case they hadn't offered me the position as president of the bank and so I wasn't too heart-broken at leaving. Not when I could play in a band at

61

the beach where I could go swimming and fishing, which Mama and I liked to do. Then it would also get Mama away from the house and its memories which I thought would be a good thing.

The days passed quickly and the little band started the summer season which was to prove the most wonderful summer – I suppose one of the happiest I ever had. My mother was carefree for the first time in her life and the boys all liked her very much. Sometimes the lady who owned the large house in which we stayed threw a party for the boys and we would have a great time. I had never seen my mother laugh so much and that made everything worthwhile as far as I was concerned. How happy I was to be a full time musician – and it was an experience that proved invaluable to me at such an early age.

Summer was gone all too soon and each day had seemed better than the last – that was in the days when 'smog' was only used in connection with orange groves when there was a frost and they had to put out the 'smudge pots' to protect the fruit on the trees.

So back to Los Angeles we went to our house in Belvedere. Just Mama and me. But almost immediately I had an offer to open at a very swanky restaurant in Los Angeles called Marcels. It was a place frequented by film stars and this sounded exciting to me. I had never seen many movie stars and the money offered was even better than I had been making at the beach, so I accepted.

I was happy I had an offer so quickly as I was now taking care of my mother and this solved the problem. The band opened and the pianist was quite a bit older than I was, but he was an awfully nice guy and we became good friends. His wife was very nice too and as it was the first time I had ever been inside such a classy joint, Bert – his name was Bert Fiske – would put me right about anything I didn't know about. He was more like a big brother and I admired his piano playing very much indeed. He was an excellent musician. When I first saw movie stars like William S Hart and Pauline Frederick come into the place to eat and dance to our music I was overawed. Just to think I was looking at the greatest of all the cowboys in person. And one of the finest actresses of her day – Pauline Frederick. We had been playing there for a few months when the band had an offer to go to San Francisco to work at a place called Marquards, a well known nightery. It meant leaving my mother alone for a time, but she finally allowed me to go with the promise from Bert that he would keep his eyes on me. She trusted Bert to keep me out of mischief. Anyway, the job was only for three months and I was excited about going on my first trip away from home.

Bert and I drove to San Francisco in his car and we shared a room at a small hotel. The band opened and I was beginning to feel like a man of the world being on my own, and one morning (about noon) when Bert and I were having breakfast at the drug store across the street from the hotel, I sat next to a very pretty girl. She was quite young and when she asked me to pass the sugar I somehow felt that here was a girl who could make me feel right at home in San Francisco – and, of course, less lonely. I really hadn't all that much experience with the other sex as yet, and I didn't know just how to navigate in these 'foreign waters', but almost before I knew it this girl solved that problem. She asked me if I had breakfast there often and I told her I had only arrived a few days before and that I was in the band at Marquards. I noticed Bert watching us. But this good Samaritan told me she would meet me there the next morning at noon for breakfast, then she would show me around. That she did! Even to taking me to her apartment to listen to some new records! The apartment was very nice indeed and, as she was not much older than me, I thought she must have a very wealthy family to be able to afford it. She asked me if I'd like to dance with her and when I put my arm around her, 'Ukulele Ike' had never sounded better as we danced to his singing of *Give Me a June Night, The Moonlight and You.* This girl was positively making me feel right at home and, before I realized the wonderment of it all, she taught me what boys and girls were all about! This I considered was a most marvellous way to be friends with someone, and 'Ike' sounded better and better with every passing moment.

She said she often went to Marquards and would come in to see me real soon. The very next night there she was. Her companion was a very large guy who turned out to be a Russian. I went over to their table and after being introduced I noticed this fellow was calling her by endearing names which made me feel a bit jealous. After all – hadn't she and I been more than just friends? But later, when I mentioned this little thing, she said she supposed he thought he had a right to call her nice names because he had proved his wonderful friendship by paying the rent for her apartment – and only a real good friend would do that.

This seemed quite a nice gesture to me on his part and as he was away for long spells (he was an officer on a ship) I helped this beautiful maiden spend many happy hours which otherwise would have been very lonesome for her. In fact, I fell violently in love with her and when I told Bert we were going to get married I noticed a look of surprise on his face. He tried to explain in the nicest way that he did not think she was quite the right kind of a girl for me, and thanks to his tact, we just remained good friends.

But the very next day my mother was knocking on my door at the hotel and I was installed in an apartment with her. She soon put me right about the whole affair (she knew just what to say in matters of this kind) and the more I saw my love-life out with her Russian sailor-boy, the more I did my best to avoid the terrible trap I had almost succumbed to. And although my heart was slightly dented, I braved the ordeal of trying to analyse the situation sensibly. I eventually came to the conclusion this girl wasn't all she should be.

Back at Marcels again where the proprietor had asked us to return, we were greeted by the people who had liked our band before we went away, and a movie actor Lew Cody (a man about town) used to come in quite often and one night he asked the boys in the band if we would like to go with him on a serenading trip out to Hollywood. He explained what it was all about and as soon as we were through work, Lew called some taxi cabs and we all piled into them and drove out to a top director's house in Beverly Hills. His name was Alan Dwan and when we arrived we sneaked over the huge lawn to just under his window and, although it was around three o'clock in the morning, we started to play some music. Immediately the lights went on in the house and Alan stuck his head out of a window and soon we were all inside the house telephoning other movie stars to come right over for a party. No sooner said than done! The house was full of a great many people I had been seeing in pictures and I was in heaven. I couldn't believe my eyes – playing for the stars! And the party went on until it was nearly time for the people to have to go to work at the film studios.

After that this was a common occurrence. Each time

Lew Cody came into Marcels he would take the gang and me out to someone's home in Hollywood or Beverly Hills and the party would begin. This, of course, caused my mother a great deal of worry as it was almost impossible to telephone her to tell her I would be late, and she was always sure I had been killed until I showed up at about six or seven in the morning. But life really began to swing for me then. To be near all those stars was something I couldn't believe.

Whenever I saw Letha and Frances I had to tell them both everything that had happened and whom I had seen, and each of them told me about the boys they had been out with, but this didn't seem to make as much difference as it might have at one time. Maybe we were growing away from each other?

One night two men came into Marcels and I noticed they both kept watching me while I played, and after a while the head-water came over and told me the two men wanted me to come to their table. I went over and they introduced themselves; one was a very famous dance-band leader, Max Fisher, and the other one said his name was Mike Lyman. I knew he was a well-known night-club entertainer and he said 'Kid, I like the way you play that trumpet and I am opening the finest night-club in the country at Santa Monica. I'm going to call it The Sunset Inn, and I'm bringing my brother Abe Lyman out from Chicago to form the greatest band ever. It will be an all star combination – so how would you like to join us?' I nearly fell off my chair but tried not to let him know. That was how I joined up with the world famous Abe Lyman Orchestra. I was seventeen years old at the time. The all-time-great Miff Mole was also brought out to the coast from Chicago to play the trombone along with Gussie Miller (clarinet with the original Dixieland Jazz Band).

Ray Lopez (my side-kick) joined the band and he was one of the very first really great white jazz cornet players. He originated the idea of using a hat or tin can over the end of his horn (which he played left-handed) and he invented several different kinds of mutes, some of them having a kazoo stuck in the end of them. He was really terrific! He handled the jazz and I played 'sweet', and when he and Miff and Gussie 'busked' a few choruses it was something I'll never forget.

Gus Arnheim (who later became one of the top bands in America when he played with his own orchestra in the Cocoanut Grove in the Ambassador Hotel in Hollywood) was our pianist. Then there was Buster Johnson, another wonderful trombone player, who wrote one of the all-time jazz classics while in the band, called *Wang Wang Blues*. Of course, Abe Lyman played drums and he was a terrific showman. He would juggle his drum sticks while playing, which always amused the dancers.

Sure enough Mike Lyman kept his word. The Sunset Inn *was* the greatest! I am convinced there can never again be anything to begin to compare with it. Mary Pickford – Douglas Fairbanks – Charlie Chaplin – Buster Keaton – Mable Normand – Rosco 'Fatty' Arbuckle – Bebe Daniels – Harold Lloyd – Rudolf Valentino, just to name only some of the stars you could meet on the dance floor any night of the week, having a lot of fun when Hollywood was still a very small town. And if I had been in heaven on seeing William S Hart for the first time, you can imagine my feeling when I was actually seeing and talking to stars who would outshine any that were to follow.

Wednesday night was 'Movie Night', and you just had to see it to believe it. The stars would always put on their own floor show. They would get on to the dance floor in front of the band and do some kind of an act, generally anything that came to mind on the spur of the moment. Buster Keaton was always good for terrific laughs with his knock-about comedy. Then 'Fatty' Arbuckle would generally join in and help tear the place apart. Mike Lyman tried to look happy, but I'm sure he experienced near heart failure on most 'Movie Nights'! The decor was beautiful and the room was filled with great large sun-flowers which created a most dazzling effect. You can just imagine what Keaton did to those sun-flowers!

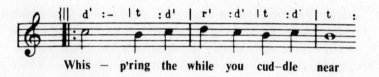

Whis — p'ring the while you cud-dle near

6. 'Whispering'

I GUESS IT was a rather strange way I was initiated into
playing my 'whispering' trumpet style for the first time.
Marshall Neilan, one of the finest and best paid film
directors, would dance by the band. He was a great
'kidder', especially when he noticed a very young
musician in the band. At the time I had a habit of
standing with my hand on my hip. It seemed quite
comfortable that way and Neilan noticed this. I didn't
realize at the time and hadn't the experience to know
that this was a common gesture of some of the queer
boys. Neilan was well conversant with that sort of thing
and as he and his girl friend danced by the band he
would put his hand on his hip and stand right in front
of me.

Ray Lopez, my side-kick, recognized what he was
driving at and told me. Well, I was quite a peaceful kid
but this annoyed me to a great extent – so much, in
fact, that I rose out of my chair, grabbed Mr Neilan by
the coat collar and quietly explained to him that the
next time he wanted to be amusing at my expense he
would be minus a couple of teeth! I don't suppose I
have ever heard anyone laugh so loud in my life. He

said, 'Kid, I just wanted to see how much you could take,' and I had the pleasure of letting him know. As soon as the dance was finished he came back to the bandstand and invited me over to his table for a drink, and when I told him I was seventeen years old he said I'd better have a Coca Cola.

Seventeen was considered pretty young in those days, I guess. Still, it was all I wanted because I had tried a sip of whisky and hadn't liked it, nor did I appreciate gin. Then Neilan said he really liked the way I played my trumpet and why didn't I bring my horn to his table and play for him? I thought this was a peculiar thing to do but I asked Abe if it would be all right and when I went back to the table I sat down and started to play, with Gus Arnheim at the small piano which could be shoved around the floor. I had played only a few notes when Mr Neilan stopped me and said it was much too loud.

He asked me if I had a mute to soften it a bit. I brought back a mute that had come with the trumpet, I put it in the horn and tried again, but he said it was still a little loud. So I stuffed the mute way up into my horn and played very quietly, and when he heard this he said that was the way I should always play. From that moment on each time he ever came to the Inn he would have me over to the table to play for him and his friends, not forgetting, of course, to hand me more money than I had seen for a while. That money I would give to Abe Lyman for the 'kitty'.

I guess I didn't tell you about the 'kitty'. I first heard about this when Mike Lyman came in to hear me that first night at Marcels. When he offered me the job he said he would give me fifty dollars a week plus an even split of the 'kitty'. The 'kitty'? I asked him what the 'kitty' was. He laughed and explained that it was a little box kept on the bandstand and every time we would play a short dance, if anyone wanted more, then they would raise their hand or let Abe Lyman know in some other way that they would put money in the 'kitty'. This all sounded too complicated to my young ears and, after consideration, I told him I would accept the fifty dollars each week but I wasn't too sure about the 'kitty' he was talking about. Again he laughed and said he would make me a proposition. He would pay me the fifty and I would let *him* have my share of the 'kitty' each week. This sounded fair enough to me; at least I was sure of my salary, so we settled it.

Following our first week of playing at the Inn, Mike called all the boys into the office that Sunday night after work. Abe had the 'kitty' box in his hand and Mike opened it and spread all the money out on his desk. I knew I had seen all those people putting money into the box, sometimes may be a hundred dollars at a time, but I certainly did not realize it would amount to this much. Mike started to count it and as soon as he finished he handed each member of the band his share and it made me start to wonder what this was all about. I asked Mike and he reminded me of our conversation at Marcels when he had offered me my fifty dollar salary *and* a split of the 'kitty' which I had refused. He was only too happy to accept my share! And he thanked me very much! He saw I looked puzzled and not to drag out the misery too long he told me that he had only been joking and handed me my share, which amounted to one hundred and twenty-five dollars, including my salary! I collected a like amount every week I stayed at The Sunset Inn and, inasmuch as I was still living at home in Los Angeles with my mother, I began riding round in my own Model T Ford Coupe within a couple of days. Just the thing to get me back

and forth from work! And the feel of having a Model T
Ford at your command! Each time I passed our old
restaurant I wondered just how many tips I would have
had to collect waiting on table to have a fine car like
this. Yes, life was good! News reached the boys in our
band that a new band was to open at the Alexandria
Hotel in Los Angeles. The leader was going to be a
fiddle player from Santa Barbara, a small town near
Hollywood, and none of us had ever heard of him. His
name was Paul Whiteman. We heard that their opening
would be a very late affair, so it gave some of the guys
in our band and myself a chance to go to hear them
after we had finished work at the Inn. We arrived just
in time to hear the last few numbers they played and to
our amazement we heard something that not only
rivalled our music, but was a little bit better! Whiteman
had a bunch of first class musicians and the band was
playing some rather advanced orchestrations. We knew
then we would have to look to our laurels and our
rehearsals were stepped up a bit. Paul Whiteman
started to make records soon after this and I even
bought some of them to play on the new Victrola I
bought Mama. I was right about his arrangements;
they were wonderful – maybe a little ahead of their
time.

I can remember well one of the very first recordings
Paul ever made with his original band. It was a tune
that had just been written by a friend of mine, Johnny
Schonberger, a young violinist who was playing at the
famous Ship Cafe which was situated on the pier at
Venice, California – a beach resort near Santa Monica.
In later years this same pier housed the ballroom where
Ben Pollock and his band were to play. This was the
band in which some of the finest young musicians like
Benny Goodman and Glenn Miller were rapidly

making a name for themselves. This melody which Johnny had just composed was played by the small band at the Ship Cafe (a replica of a pirate ship) and it became very popular, not only with the crowds that frequented the place, but with other band-leaders who heard this beautiful tune and wanted to play it. Johnny immediately realized he had written a string of notes thay may have a chance of being published if he could get someone to write a lyric for them. There was a well known lyric writer around Los Angeles named Dick Coburn, and Johnny approached him to see if he would be interested in writing some words for his tune. Dick came up with a very simple lyric which was in keeping with this lovely melody – and he called it *Whispering*. I mention this story because this song was later to play a big part in my career.

Since those early days Johnny and I have retained our friendship which I have always valued highly. He later played in the Abe Lyman Orchestra for years, quite some time after I had left it, and a few years later he came to London and paid me a visit. He was a bit older but still a very nice guy. Johnny had never heard my British band and only a few days ago I sent him a tape of my last recording of *Whispering* which I recorded in about 1937. I sent it to him to his home in North Hollywood where he is residing. I still hear from him quite often and I'm sure he will never regret the day he took a small piece of manuscript paper, scribbled some notes and called them *Whispering*.

Mexico was just a few hours drive in a car from Hollywood and every weekend many of the picture people would go there for the horse-racing and a flutter in the Casino. So much were they in a hurry to lose their money, that on numerous occasions several of them had been picked up for speeding through Santa

Anna, a small town on the way. Finally, a judge issued a statement saying the next time anyone from Hollywood was caught speeding, he would personally see to it they were entertained at the expense of the local government – in jail! He thought he could probably accommodate them for at least a month. Well, it happened one day that this beautiful young actress was driving faster than the judge thought necessary and she landed in jail. Everyone in Hollywood heard about it and our band decided to go to Santa Anna and cheer her up a bit with some music. We arrived there. The jail-house was a tiny brick building in the middle of a large square, surrounded with lawn – quite a nice setting. As quietly as possible we made our way to just under her cell window and struck up *The Prisoner's Song*. It only took a moment for her to appear at the window and the next thing we knew, we were all in her cell having a party. We were surprised to learn she had her mother staying with her as 'house guest', and her own bedroom suite for comfort! That outstandingly beautiful actress was Bebe Daniels. I believe Bebe had the flashingest big brown eyes I'd seen. She was Harold Lloyd's leading lady and when she was leaving, the judge presented her with a large bouquet of roses just to show there were no hard feelings.

One night at The Sunset Inn, Marshall Neilan came in for a dance and some food, and during the evening he asked me if I would like to come to the studio where he was directing Mary Pickford in *Rebecca of Sunnybrook Farm*. Micky and I had become good friends and I felt thrilled at the prospect of watching him direct the world's number one motion picture star in one of her most outstanding films, especially when I myself had a hidden desire to become a movie director one day. I still don't know how I missed out on it as I did have the opportunities if I had only taken them. Maybe it was because I started making so much money with my trumpet. It was difficult to think of giving up all the things I was able to buy with my new found wealth, when it would mean working as 'property boy' or some such job just to get a start in the picture business. But I really think I have been just a little sorry I didn't take the step at that time. And, of course, I couldn't have bought my nice brand-new Model T Ford Coupe, which was the apple of my eye, with the bright shiny red wire wheels! But although I have been on hundreds of movie sets since, and have appeared in numerous films with my band, I think I got just about the biggest kick out of sitting next to Micky Neilan under a large umbrella (to keep the sun out of our eyes) near the camera-man while Mary Pickford did some of her scenes. This, of course, was a silent picture and at that time they generally had music played by a few musicians on the side-lines to give atmosphere to the actors – quite often when they were going to do a cry scene. It would help the star get into the mood. After that wonderful experience I was thankful I hadn't punched Micky Neilan on the nose.

While still at The Sunset Inn I could look out of the window down onto the pier at Santa Monica where my mother and I used to go fishing when I was very young. We both loved to go there for a day's fishing and many a time we would be waiting for a 'bite' when all of a sudden we would hear a great splash in the sea, which generally meant a Mack Sennett movie crew was out on the end of the pier and the splash was caused by Ford Sterling and the Keystone Cops falling into the water while chasing Al St John or some other 'baddie'. Sometimes it would be 'Fatty' Arbuckle they were try-ing to catch. This type of thing was nearly an everyday occurrence and very often my mother and I would take time off from fishing to go onto the sand and watch Marie Dressler making one of her earlier films. It seemed the beach was a favourite place to make movies as no sets were needed, saving a great deal of expense. Many of the early two reel comedies were made on location on the beach at a place which is now known as Malibu. And little did I think when pulling out a mackerel one day that I would be in one of America's top bands playing my trumpet, right up there on the Palisades overlooking the pier. Just about this time Mike Lyman was going to open another night-club in Los Angeles to be called The Palais Royal and a band-leader, Henry Halstead, was getting a band together to play there. He made me an offer which was even better than I was getting with Abe Lyman, so I accepted it. The room was completely decorated in pleated linen material making the acoustics the best I have ever worked in anywhere. It helped keep the music very quiet which appealed to me and we played to many of the same stars who went to The Sunset Inn, and the place was an over-night success. Gloria Swanson was there nearly every night along with Cecil B De Mille and the 'Who's Who' of show business. I wondered if they both realized that here I was sitting in the band playing for their listening and dancing pleasure, and it was I who had, on one of my first 'personal appearances', been responsible for the bugle calls which brought absolute quiet on the set when my lungs practically exploded with the force of a tornado as I calmly gave Mr De Mille the silence he desired.

One night as I was passing the table where Mike Lyman was sitting with Gloria Swanson, he stopped me and asked me to sit with them and introduced me to Miss Swanson. But I refrained from reminding her about the day I had thought of so many times, and which I had related to nearly everyone I met, because I realized it had taken place a few years ago, and I also knew beautiful actresses did not like to *think* about a few years ago. Gloria was one of the Mack Sennett Bathing Beauties in 1916. She had a very wide range in acting. One of her greatest screen performances was in Billy Wilder's *Sunset Boulevard*.

But having the chance to be sitting right next to this great star was almost too much. I think the first thing I noticed was her nose turned up on the end. Just enough to make it the nicest nose I had seen in many a day. All of a sudden I liked noses. And then I got a whiff of that perfume! If the guys who went to see her on the screen could have inhaled this unbelievable fragrance – I'm sure they would have been that much more ardent. When I was called back to the bandstand by a special emissary especially sent by Henry Halstead, it was most difficult to tear myself away from this wonderful floating sensation I was experiencing. At that moment I was sorry I had ever taken up trumpet playing. But, gracefully excusing myself, I made my way back to where Henry was waiting to play the next dance set and he very nicely thanked me for condescending to join the band again – he was sorry for the interruption. Well, I don't think I had ever played so 'sweetly' before.

It was while I was 'giving out' with one of my soft delectable solos when I looked up and saw a vision of loveliness. I was always looking up at visions of loveliness! But this one was something to be marvelled at. She had lovely eyes and a smile that made me 'fluff' a couple of notes, and a body to match. In a brief moment I found I was not quite as interested now in Gloria Swanson as I had been a few minutes before, as this beautiful girl was positively just the kind of girl I had been looking for – sort of 'out of this world'! How could I have allowed Gloria to affect my feelings the way she did when there was someone like this dancing before my very eyes? It took me the best part of ten minutes before I was talking to her in the foyer and this gal strictly had class. I let her know I was perfectly willing to ring her any time she would like and that wasn't going to be until the next day. I tried to keep my mind on my playing for the rest of the evening and the outcome of the telephone call was the beginning of a very happy romance with Helen Thomas. Helen was one of the Al Christie Girls. Al Christie owned his own studio on Sunset Boulevard in Hollywood where he made the famous Christie Comedies, and the Christie Girls were on a par with the Mack Sennett Bathing Beauties. Well, Helen and I started going around together and she used to invite me out to the studio when she was working. There one would see many of the now famous comedians falling on their backsides or being the recipients of a custard pie. Helen had been keeping company with a young fighter by the name of Joe Benjamin (he'd just won a title) and I was wondering at which moment he would let me 'have it', but I finally won out in the end – intact. Joe Benjamin was a pal of Jack Dempsey and maybe the fact that I knew Dempsey by this time helped a bit.

Henry Halstead's band was making quite a reputation and was starting to become known throughout the States. We even had offers to go to New York, but all that California sunshine was hard to give up. While with the band I was beginning to get other offers and everything was rosy. Then one day I heard that a young millionaire oil-man was to build a night-club in Culver City, near Metro-Goldwyn-Mayer Studios. Naturally he was going to need a dance band, so who better than Roy Fox to lead it? Yes, not a bad idea at all! So I made my way down to Culver City to see him and when I met Bill Hollifield he looked like a college boy. He was a very nice guy and his young wife was a lovely person. I don't think he knew how much he was worth, so obviously that was how he could afford to build this beautiful club, surrounded by landscaped gardens. I can say it was the most wonderful looking place I've ever seen.

Anyway, I convinced him I was the one to supply the music, so when I was twenty years old I had my first big band. I talked him into letting me have my name outside the club in electric lights and after our opening night everyone was talking about the Club Royale and Roy Fox and his band. The band was highly successful and our 'floor-show' consisted of such names as Sophie Tucker and Marion Harris (one of the greatest singers I have ever heard; she was the top recording star of her time) and her accompanist was J Russell Robinson, the pianist with the original Dixieland Jazz Band.

You had to see Marion Harris on the cabaret floor or on the stage to appreciate the fact that her artistry was something to marvel at both as a singer and in the way she put over a song. This was proved years later when she opened at the Cafe de Paris in London (where my band was playing) in 1930. She took London by storm. Royalty and society flocked to see and hear her. But more of that later. We also played the great Palace Theatre on Broadway together – but again I'm getting ahead of my story.

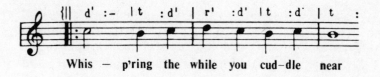

Whis — p'ring the while you cud-dle near

7. My First Band

ONE NIGHT HELEN Thomas came into the Club Royale with my best pal. He used to bring her in to see me and they would dance while waiting for me to finish playing; then I'd drive her home. It was nice having a friend who would do that for you and I really appreciated it, but then I would do the same for him. He even went further than this. He had had a fair amount of experience with women and knew just how much worry they could cause you sometimes, so to prove his friendship, he married Helen that same evening, just so I wouldn't run into any of that kind of trouble with her. And the nice part was he came down especially to tell me my worries were over!

Just down the road from our club was a late-night club called The Green Mill. The place looked like a movie set – a large water-mill was turning, powered by water from a 'stream' with arc lights playing on the place. It was designed by someone from one of the studios and was a show place. Later the name was changed to The Cotton Club and that's where I first met the great Louis Armstrong. Louis's band was playing there and, as they closed later than we did, it gave me the chance to hear Louis many times and we became good friends. Of course, I had heard him on records, but you just had to see him to believe his showmanship, aside from his great trumpet playing and unusual singing style. This was only matched by his wonderful personality. I didn't know it then, but our paths were to cross more than once in later years.

Sometimes Louis would come to the Club Royale to hear my band and after I had been playing there for nearly a year I went to visit a friend of mine who had just arrived from New York, Jack Mills, a music publisher. He was stopping at the Biltmore Hotel in Los Angeles, which had only opened that very same day, and when I walked into his room he said, 'Sophie Tucker is staying at the hotel so let's ring her and ask her in for a drink.' So he got on the 'phone and when I spoke to her she asked me what I was doing in the hotel. I told her I had come to see Jack and she said she was wondering why I wasn't down at the Club Royale when it was burning! I said, 'You're kidding', and she explained she had just heard it on the radio. Of course, you can imagine my surprise when I arrived at the club to find the entire building in ashes – burnt to the ground! All our instruments, uniforms and, above all, our jobs gone! It was a real heart-breaker, and quite by accident. The Biltmore Hotel was to have had its official opening night within a few days time. Their resident band was to be the Art Hickman orchestra. His band was going to play in the ball-room that first night and, when the management heard about the Club Royale burning, they asked me to play in the Supper Room with my band, just for the opening. I did this but it meant there was no other job available for my gang at such short notice. When Art Hickman heard this he asked me if I would consider joining his orchestra on trumpet. He had been very famous as a band-leader at the Palace Hotel in San Francisco where he made his big reputation on radio, playing in the Rose Room.

By this time Art Hickman had been in the band business for quite some time and felt he was getting on a bit, so he accepted an offer by the management of the Biltmore to become Head of Entertainment for the hotel group, so Art retired from the musical end and became an executive. He put Earl Burtnett in charge of the orchestra. Earl was an excellent pianist and a well-known song writer, so after much consideration I decided to join up with him. It was really a fine orchestra and by this time the orchestrations for big bands were getting better and better. Earl Burtnett himself was a very good arranger and he was one of the nicest people I have ever met in the band business. It was a lovely room we played in and we broadcast every night. Just to give you an idea how intimate radio was in the beginning, there was a telephone on the band-stand next to Earl's piano and he could receive outside calls from a public requesting tunes while we were playing. We had our own special operator at the switch-board to handle the calls.

Often while at the Biltmore some of the boys in the band and I would walk across the street during a break to get some fresh air in a park directly opposite the hotel. I had rather a soft spot for this little park (it was only one block square), for it was one of the places at which I had played while I was with the Los Angeles Examiner Newsboys' Band at a Festival being held in the park which had a small bandstand in the centre. There were fireworks and clowns plus beautiful girls dressed in costume and the whole thing was very exciting for me. At our rehearsal we had practised playing a new song that had been written by a song-writer from

New York who was in Los Angeles at the time, and he was going to appear at the Festival conducting our band while we played his song. He even sang it through a megaphone to the large crowd. His voice wasn't very good but it didn't seem to stop the song from becoming a big hit. It was one of the very first 'rag-time' pieces I had ever played and it was called *Alexander's Ragtime Band*. I'm glad Irving Berlin was a good song-writer for I'm very much afraid he wouldn't have made it as a crooner!

But back to the Biltmore where our band became so popular on radio. It wasn't long before we were asked by Victor Records to do some recording for them. In the early days there were no recording studios in Los Angeles so the record company always had to bring all their equipment out to the coast from New York. I shall never forget the very first record I ever made. It's hard to believe now but Victor hired a suite of rooms at the Alexandria Hotel where, as I said earlier, Paul Whiteman was playing with his band, and when we arrived to record we were ushered into the suite and in the drawing-room a great big horn was sticking out of the wall which divided it from the bedroom. The horn was about six or seven feet long. At that time they hadn't started to use microphones and if anyone wanted to play a solo they would have to stand right in front of this large horn and blow right into it. Even to get a good cymbal crash the cymbal had to be held almost inside. This recording idea was something quite new to me and I can still remember being very nervous. Although I have since made close on to two thousand records, the very first one is the one which sticks out in my memory. Many of the motion picture stars came to the Biltmore to dance to our music, and one night I had the great pleasure of seeing a really terrific looking girl dancing in front of the band. So I took a chance and smiled at her. Well, to my utter amazement she returned the smile and it didn't take long before I arranged to take her out. She was the sister of Marie Prevost, one of the Mack Sennett Bathing Beauties, and her name was Peggy Prevost. She was also in films, so our chance meeting blossomed into a long term engagement. We went to many movie parties together and one evening we arranged to pick up Sam Warner in my car to take him and his wife to a party in Beverley Hills given by Peggy's sister Marie. I remember Sam telling me on the way about the new idea he had for films that talked. Sam died somewhere about this time, so Jack Warner, his brother, continued with the idea. But more of that later.

That night at the party I met one of the nicest people I had ever met in show-business – Lon Chaney, who was in comedies initially and was with William S Hart in Westerns. His role in *The Hunchback of Notre Dame* was followed by *The Phantom of the Opera*. He was, in fact, one of the most quietly spoken men and you would never have thought he could horrify you in some of the parts he played in his many great pictures. Another very nice guy who was at the party was named Victor Schertzinger, one of the big film directors, and he was sitting at the piano playing a song he had composed called *Marquita,* and quite by chance I happened to have my trumpet in my car so we wound up playing his tune together.

Marie Prevost had the usual beautiful swimming pool in her garden and it was graced by the Mack Sennett Beauties and, of course, I did my best not to let Peggy know how much I enjoyed the proceedings. Zazu Pitts was a great friend of Marie Prevost and was very funny in the pool. Hollywood was such a happy place in those carefree days, and night after night there were parties. Not the kind of parties you could read about in some of the scandal sheets, but real good fun. One afternoon Peggy and I were invited down to Malibu Beach, before it became too publicised. A barbecue was given by a friend who owned a most marvellous beach house built like a ranch house. It was in the hills just next to the sea and was quite a place. We all dressed in Western gear and when we arrived we saw a great big ox or cow or whatever it is they barbeque, roasting away over a large pit of embers. I've never tasted such meat!

Then, as evening closed in, my friends had engaged a 'cowboy' orchestra to play for dancing in a small pavilion and, needless to say, there were plenty of picture people there. That was the first time I met Rudolph Valentino. When I was still quite a kid someone told me I looked like Valentino and I wore out several mirrors looking at myself. I couldn't actually see the resemblance when we met, but he was a very nice person. I fancied myself as a pretty good dancer and he showed me some of his favourite steps while doing the tango, which he was famous for. But I didn't think I would ever win any trophies with my tango and I'm sure he agreed.

By this time I was getting a bit restless at not having my own band, but out of a clear blue sky I had an offer to form a band and open at a new place called the Lafayette Cafe, half way between Los Angeles and Hollywood. It was a beautiful room and catered for a very smart clientele. It was great to be back band-leading and through my broadcasts we were well on our way again.

We played in quite a number of films when music was wanted for a night-club scene, and this work, intermingled with the movie parties we played, made it all very worthwhile financially. At about this time, a rather strange thing happened. One evening I was called over to a table where a man was sitting, and I had noticed he had been in several times listening to the music and especially watching me. Well, he introduced himself and asked me if I would consider becoming his partner in a new club-restaurant he was expecting to open in Hollywood. He said that if I would join him in this venture I didn't have to put up any money (which delighted me), but if he could use my name as host and my music, he would assure me the place would be the very finest spot in Hollywood. He asked me to show him where he could purchase a new car (later I took him to a friend in the motor-car business), and then he asked me to try to find a good location for our new room. I found a terrific location on Hollywood Boulevard and we had the decorators in (the walls were to be hung in silk), and the kitchen outfitters were planning that end of it. I also found him a chauffeur for the car. Then, one day I was called out to his hotel in Beverly Hills and was taken up to his suite by the manager and there on the bed was this man being held down by two attendants – stark raving MAD!

Peggy Prevost was coming in to see me quite often, and I made it a point not to let her be with one of my best friends! I found I wasn't missing Helen as much as I thought I should, so maybe my pal had done me a favour. Yes, Peggy was quite terrific.

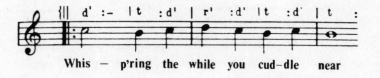

Whis — p'ring the while you cud–dle near

8. Miami

THE OWNER OF the Lafayette decided to put in Cabaret
and the first artiste he engaged was Marion Harris.
Marion and I had become good friends while working
together at the Club Royale and she was pleased to
know my band was there. Again she was a tremendous
hit and stayed several weeks. Harry, the guy who owned
the joint, wanted her to remain longer but she had
made arrangements to open in Vaudeville and asked
me if I would like to join her act. It meant that she
wanted me to direct the 'pit' orchestra in the theatres
and, while she was making a change of costume, I was
to play a trumpet solo in my quiet style – later to
become known as my 'Whispering' trumpet. J Russell
Robinson was still her accompanist on the piano and,
inasmuch as Marion said there would be quite a lot of
travelling over the Orpheum Circuit (the name of the
theatre chain extending all over the States), I decided to
give up the band, as this kind of life seemed to be rather
exciting. I talked it over with Harry and, as we were
very good friends, he understood my feeling and said
that if I would like to accept the offer I could always
return if there was an opening. He did ask me to find

him another band to take my place while I was away; so I took a trip down to a seaside resort called Balboa Beach, to a dance hall where I had previously noticed a drummer with a terrific personality in the small band. He had a wonderful smile and sang a great song. A pretty good looking guy too.

Yes, it was Phil Harris, and when I went back and told the Cafe proprietor about Phil, he engaged him and another musician to form a band which was called the Loughner-Harris orchestra, and that was the start of the long success Phil Harris has enjoyed in show-business.

Well, I opened the tour with Marion Harris at the Orpheum Theatre in San Francisco and it really did turn out to be exciting! Hearing the applause after I had played my solo was most thrilling – quite different from when I was playing with my band for dancing. All eyes were glued on me and it took quite some time before I started to become used to the idea. I remember it was Thanksgiving Day and the theatre was closed for the day. Marion, Russell and I felt rather lonesome at not being at home for our big turkey dinner with our families but, as luck would have it, we were all invited out to join a very nice family at their home for dinner. It was most welcome!

I continued to work with Marion on the West Coast until one day she was taken ill with throat trouble. This meant I was out of a job, at least for the time being, so what was I to do? Luck came my way again rather surprisingly. Earl Burtnett who was still leading the Art Hickman orchestra at the Biltmore Hotel, asked me if I would like to go to Miami, Florida, with him. By this time he had taken over the Hickman Orchestra and had accepted an offer to take the band to Miami to open at the Columbus Hotel. Well, this sounded pretty good to me, for I liked the idea of more travelling and the money was exceptionally good. Earl and I had become good friends while I was with the band before, and there was a possibility, Earl said, of us going on to New York from Miami. But I sort of felt that one of the reasons I took the offer was Peggy Prevost, who by this time had been in the Ziegfeld Follies in New York, and, as I hadn't seen her for quite some time, here was a good chance to put that right. You see, Peggy was also going to Florida with the Follies at exactly the same time as I would be there. Only she was going to be in Palm Beach – not too far from Miami. This seemed rather a good idea. After rehearsing with the Burtnett band we got on our way and, to break the journey, we played an engagement at the Orpheum Theatre in New Orleans. As our band was so well known by this time through broadcasting our welcome was most gratifying.

While in New Orleans, the boys in the band and I made the rounds of some of the most famous night-clubs and we had a wonderful experience, as it was Mardi Gras week and the place was really swinging. Some of the musicians we met there took us round and we were shown spots we never would have heard about if it hadn't been for them. Once again, after meeting Louis Armstrong in Hollywood, our paths crossed. He was playing in one of the better known Clubs. Louis and I, after he had finished at the club, sat up most of one night and I listened to some of his experiences which were certainly interesting. The next day he took me to see the annual Mardi Gras parade and I do not know if the parade or Louis caused the biggest furore. He was known by everyone and was loved by all the people. And what a wonderful time I had with him! One I shall never forget.

The week we stayed in New Orleans was all too short

and we then went to San Antonio in Texas, where we had a month's engagement at the Gunter Hotel playing for dancing, before we opened in Miami. This turned out to be a most happy experience as the people there were so hospitable. On Thanksgiving Day, Earl Burtnett and I were invited to stay at the beautiful home of some people we met. We were taken up in the mountains on the night before to their cabin and brought back some wild turkey and a deer. A real Thanksgiving! One of the things I remember about San Antonio is that when you walked around the streets late at night you could hear the most marvellous music being played by a small group of coloured musicians on a street corner. Maybe a harmonica and guitar. These negroes would play the most wonderful folk-type of blues you could possibly want to hear. It was just out of this world! They, of course, couldn't read a note of music, but I can honestly say I have never heard quite anything to compare with what they played. And to make the whole thing even more delightful we would buy Hot-tamales (a very hot Mexican food) from the Hot-tamale man standing close by. I have tasted millions of tamales but never any like those, especially when the night was cold. Now it was time for the band to be on its way to Miami, Florida! What a pleasant thought because, although it was the height of winter in Texas, there was all that sunshine for us to look forward to. We travelled by train and I still think Earl Burtnett showed a profit on the trip, through teaching us a new game of cards. It all helped to pass the time as I was anxious to see Peggy again. On the way, the train passed through Palm Beach before it arrived in Miami, and when I got to Palm Beach, Peggy was waiting on the platform. She looked absolutely wonderful, as brown as a berry. Later, as we were riding along the lake-side in one of those chairs with bicycle wheels driven by a coloured man, I think the closest I have come to being seriously damaged was when a cocoanut fell from out of one of the trees lining the path we were riding along. What a noise it made while falling! This was probably more frightening than anything else. Well, we finally came to the place where the Ziegfeld Follies were playing and it was a terrific South Seas type of building. It looked like one of our Hollywood movie sets.

I went to see the show that night and, of course, it was hard for me to take my eyes off Peggy, as she was one of the show girls who had been selected from hundreds of beautiful girls by Flo Zeigfeld. He had the reputation of having nothing but beauty in his productions.

I spent a few days in Palm Beach, then had to get on my way to Miami. When I arrived there, Earl told me the opening of the hotel was delayed for a month, so there was nothing to do but swim and lie on the golden sand, fish in the Gulf Stream, and go racing at Hileah Park Race Track. I always did like a little bet, and as this was the very first time I had seen horse-racing it made it easy for me to part with my money.

Between this and the gambling casinos at night, I successfully made the people I gambled with very happy indeed. Well, the month soon passed and now for the opening of the Hotel! The room in which we played was on the roof surrounded entirely by huge glass windows overlooking the blue sea and the Gulf Stream. It was too beautiful to be true! And I don't believe I have ever seen a more distinguished crowd at any Gala Opening anywhere. The jewels! And especially, that tropical weather, not a bit like the snow we had just left in Texas.

By this time Paul Whiteman had opened with his orchestra at the Coral Gables Country Club in Miami and one night I went out to hear him, and, of course, the band was the last word musically speaking! Henry Busse was still his lead trumpet player and, just as Earl Burtnett and I had struck up a good friendship, Paul Whiteman and Busse were great friends. Busse was sort of the mainstay of the band for years and I had always considered him a pretty hot competitor when it came to trumpet playing.

One night Paul Whiteman came in to hear our band and, after a while when I had a break, I went to his table and he told me he had come in especially to hear me because he had just had a row with Henry Busse and would I be interested in joining his orchestra, taking Henry's place? I was naturally amazed at this bit of news and was rather sorry to hear it, knowing how friendly they had been. It took me so by surprise that I told him I would have to think it over and would let him know. Somehow, on the spur of the moment it seemed that if I were to take this step, it would be something I would be more tied up with than I really wanted to be, because I had had my own bands and naturally, my ultimate goal was to be my own boss again. I knew that if I joined Paul it would have to be for 'keeps' and I didn't want to walk out on him at any time when I decided to have my own band. With Earl Burtnett it was just a matter of the travel that interested me mostly and, after the Miami trip, there was the possibility of going to New York. But the Whiteman offer came to nothing, as he and Busse made it up, and, in a way, I was just as pleased to remain with Burtnett. While I was in Miami, Peggy Prevost and I saw quite a lot of each other. Then the Ziegfeld Follies closed and she went back to California. It was just about time for our band to finish our three month engagement at the hotel and Earl Burtnett and I decided to go on to New York and see what it was all about.

We went by boat and, although I am the world's worst sailor, the first day aboard was a very pleasant one for me. It so happened that a New York show had also closed after spending the season in Miami and the entire cast were on the ship. Quite by accident I met a beautiful red-head from the show and we hit it off well together. That night we both sat on the deck under one of the largest moons I'd ever seen. Maybe it only looked larger, but when I was beginning to realize life was really worthwhile, a storm blew up and that was the last I ever saw of the girl. It was the worst storm for many years and all I could do was to stay in my bed and hold on! Once I let loose and was thrown across the cabin and back again. This lasted a couple of days and, to make everything more terrible, Earl Burtnett was enjoying the whole proceedings. He was one of the happiest drinkers I knew, so he took practically no notice of anything.

We finally made it to New York and, as we neared it, the sight was one of the most thrilling things I can remember, especially as it was the first time I had been there. Those buildings! What a place – so very different from the buildings in Los Angeles and San Francisco. They were kept pretty low then on account of the earthquakes. But I was dying to get off the boat and see for myself the place I had always heard so much about. We stopped at an hotel right in the heart of Times Square and the very first things I wanted to see were the Subway (we didn't have them in California and I'd never seen one) and the Automat! This was an inexpensive type of eating place where you put coins into the slot and in return you would get the food displayed in small compartments behind little glass windows. This, at the time, was quite a novelty to me, but not to Earl Burtnett, as he had seen it all before. Of course, I had heard of the bright lights on Broadway but I had no idea there would be so many. Millions of them! All kinds of electric signs that were most entertaining. It was all unbelievable. For our first night out we went up to Harlem to the Cotton Club where we saw the most terrific floor-show. And a great coloured band. It was led by a guy named Duke Ellington.

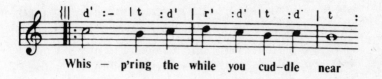

Whis — p'ring the while you cud-dle near

9. New York

ONE OF THE first things that happened to me in New York was to be invited to play at a Charity Concert at the Metropolitan Opera House. Charity Concerts were a popular form of entertainment on Sunday nights and most of the top stars appeared. Earl Burtnett went along with me to act as my accompanist. When it was our turn to go on I can vividly remember it seemed like a mile to the centre of the stage – it was so huge! I hadn't been on all that many stages before and it was nervous making. Earl reached there first as his legs were longer. But what a beautiful theatre! Just think of me playing in the Metropolitan Opera House! Well, when I finished doing my spot, the applause was very thrilling, and as I walked off stage a man in the wings stopped me and said, 'Hey, son, you're going to do all right with that horn of yours!' He was a little guy and as he was so friendly I was glad to hear his encouraging words. He was ready to go on next and as I said good-bye, the stage manager tapped me on the shoulder and asked me if I knew who that fellow was. Naturally I didn't. I hardly knew anyone in New York as yet. You can imagine my surprise when the stage manager told me it was Al Jolson. His songs were most movingly sentimental and his popularity was immense. His *The Jazz Singer* in 1927 and *The Singing Fool* in the following year marked the launching of the talkies by Warner Bros. A compliment coming from the great Jolson so early in my career made a big impression on me, especially as I had only seen him on the stage when I was a kid, in a musical called *Big Boy* when it came to Los Angeles. Then, of course, he worked in 'black-face' as he did in his productions and films, but that night at the Opera House he didn't have any make-up on. The artistes weren't allowed to use make-up or costumes on account of it being Sunday. It was the law. Knowing it was Al Jolson I went back into the wings and listened to him charm the audience, and they hardly let him leave the stage.

Earl finally went back to the West Coast to return to the Biltmore Hotel, but I stayed on in New York because I wanted to join the New York Musicians Union. You had to be resident in New York for at least six months before you could become a full member. So, what should happen but at breakfast one morning in a drug-store I saw a theatre bill announcing the opening of Marion·Harris at the Palace Theatre on Broadway the following week! The Palace was the world's number one Variety or Vaudeville theatre at that time, so off I went to find out at the stage door where I could locate Marion. Luckily she was rehearsing, and when she saw me she threw her arms around me and said it was a coincidence that I should show up as she had wondered where I was and would like me to join her during her stay at the Palace and do a spot on the stage with my trumpet while she made her change of dress, just like we did on the coast. J Russell Robinson was still with her.

You can well imagine my excitement, having the

chance of playing the world famous Palace Theatre –
the lifetime ambition of every artiste. I could hardly
wait for the opening night which finally arrived. I got
to the theatre early and Marion suggested that I put on
some make-up which had always been somewhat of a
hindrance when I used to have to use it in any of the
films I had played in. But Marion knew best and
although it made my mouthpiece slide around a bit on
my lips while playing, I knew it was essential. You see,
I didn't use make-up when we were together before as
I was playing in the pit with the orchestra.

After the very warm introduction Marion gave me
while I was waiting in the wings, the applause seemed
loud in my ears as I made my way to the centre of the
stage. I can still remember my thoughts at that moment
– as long as I can remember I have been hearing about
this very stage I am walking on. I can hardly believe it!
This stage where all the all time greats, the world's most
famous stars, had brought audiences to their feet
through their own sheer artistry. Thousands of the
cream of vaudeville acts – Al Jolson – Sophie Tucker –
Nora·Bayes – Fanny Brice – Jack Benny – Eva Tanguay
– Will Rogers – Eddie Cantor – Georgie Jessel – the
great comics – the astounding 'wire acts' – the unbelievable conjurors. And here am I walking on the
same boards that had held all those wonderful names!

Russell played my introduction on the piano and
immediately the audience were so still I could actually
hear my own heart beat. I had always been nervous
when playing before the public and this was no exception. But at the same time I do not think I have ever
been so thrilled, before or since. I have been asked on
many occasions what I thought of when I was playing
my trumpet. It was generally about a beautiful gal who
was dancing in front of the band, when I was resident

at one of the night spots; or, if in a theatre doing our stage show, I may be wondering just how I had missed that putt which had cost me the game. But just now strangely enough my mind was on that little cornet I stood looking in at the window of the second-hand store and how Mr Showalter had first taught me how to blow it. But all of a sudden I realized I had completed playing my solo and that terrific applause was for me! It was just as if I was hearing clapping for the very first time – and from the stage of the Palace Theatre, on Broadway!

This was a wonderful experience for me as my name started to get around a bit in the profession and I had excellent reviews in the Press saying how unusual it was to hear a trumpet being played so quietly. Marion slayed the audience. It was easy to understand why she was one of the top headliners in American vaudeville.

Just after I had finished my stint at the Palace, an orchestra leader got in touch with me to see if I would be interested in playing in his orchestra at a large cinema up-town. He said he would feature me playing my trumpet solos at each performance and offered me an acceptable salary. As I didn't have a lot of cash I thought it might be a good way of spending part of the remaining time before I could join the Union. So I took the job with Phil Fabello. Each week when the film was changed I would go into the audience to see the new picture, and, one time, while groping for my seat in the dark, I tripped over the feet of someone, apologised, and fell into the next seat. When my eyes became more accustomed to the darkness I noticed sitting next to me the most beautiful girl! Naturally, this called for a further apology and she was quite pleasant about it. She said she had heard me playing in the orchestra and thought my playing was very nice. She even introduced

me to her mother who was sitting next to her. I thought
the least I could do would be to invite her out to dinner
and she said she would be happy to accept. Well, that
was the start of things and we began to see a great deal
of each other. Her name was Dorothea and she told me
she was in the Marx Brothers musical show *The
Cocoanuts* playing on Broadway. She was one of the
show-girls who displayed the lovely costumes in the
production numbers. One night she invited me to see
the show and I must say she really looked terrific! When
I went back-stage she introduced me to the Marx
Brothers, who began on the vaudeville stage as children,
under the powerful influence of their mother Minnie.
Their first film was *The Cocoanuts,* then followed *Animal
Crackers, A Night at the Opera* and *A Day at the Races.* They
had fabulous success.

They were all very nice guys and I became quite
friendly with Harpo. Groucho asked Dorothea and me
out to have some food at a very popular place called
Lindy's and Harpo joined us. Harpo was a very quiet
person, while Groucho kept us all laughing. Lindy's was
the meeting place for show folk on Broadway and
Harpo pointed out many of the big stars. It was all very
exciting. Harpo said he had heard me playing at the
Palace Theatre when I was with Marion Harris and
asked me how I got such a quiet sound. I explained it
was caused by a special kind of mute I used. He said he
would like to get together with me sometime with his
harp and have a session, which we did later.

It was in his dressing-room where he generally kept
his harp that we had out first get-together. It was
during a very hot summer and to get a breath of air he
left the dressing-room door open and, although we were
playing quietly, we soon had an audience of some of the
stagehands who were in the theatre at the time and

some of the kids in the chorus. Harpo and I got along very well together. First he would ask me if I remembered a certain tune which we would play, then I would recall a melody for our fast-growing repertoire. Then there were the requests from our delighted audience, followed by a certain amount of applause. Harpo and I got together on several occasions and he really enjoyed busking some of the oldies. I certainly did too as he was such a nice guy and a natural born musician. I remember one day he sent out for ice-cold drinks for the gang, which helped my blowing considerably. That was on one of the hotter days and believe me when I say that summer New York weather can make your mouth awfully dry – which doesn't aid blowing a horn. But it was all real good fun and something I enjoy remembering.

About this time I heard that Sophie Tucker was opening in her own room 'Sophie Tucker's Playground' right in the heart of New York. Inasmuch as I knew Sophie, having worked with her, I took Dorothea to the opening, and during the evening Sophie came to our table to say Hello and asked me what I was doing in New York. I told her and she bought us a drink before she did her cabaret act. Teddy Shapiro, her accompanist, had been with her for years and he also came over to the table to say Hello. Of course, when he struck up Sophie's introduction *Some of these Days,* you would have thought the roof was coming down. I have never heard more applause! She was loved by the New York crowd and I'm sure she could have sung all night if they'd had their way. This was all during prohibition and these clubs were generally backed by some of the leading citizens – gangsters! But they had a lot of money to spend and could pay the artistes well to appear in cabaret.

During the evening I didn't pay much attention to the fact that Dorothea and I had a couple of cocktails upon arrival but during dinner she suggested we had another bottle of wine. Anything to please so beautiful a lady, and while we danced she grew less and less steady on her pretty feet! As it was getting late I thought it may be well to get her out into the air, so I suggested we walk up Broadway and look in the windows for a while. Dorothea liked the idea. We were walking along having a few laughs and all of a sudden she started telling me off about some trivial matter. I thought it was rather cute having this lovely person angry at me for no reason at all. After a short time she started to feel better and said how sorry she was. She didn't know what had come over her, she said, and, of course, I didn't give it a second thought. I was too happy just being with her. Anyone could feel out of sorts after a few drinks. We started seeing a lot of each other until she had to go on the road with the Marx Brothers' show.

Before long someone contacted me at the cinema where I was still working, and asked me to come to see them at a certain address, which I did. This man also said he had heard me at the Palace Theatre and would I like to put my own band into his new Club (which, of course, meant a 'speakeasy'). He offered me money which was hard to refuse, and it meant having my own band again, so I accepted. The place was at 54th and Broadway. Phil Fabello talked me into remaining at the cinema with him, as my job in the Club didn't start until eleven o'clock at night. We played until six am, so it really turned out to be not too much sleep for me. In this small room we had a few cabaret acts, and one was a sleek-haired young dancer who did a jazz dance called the *Black Bottom* and that was the first time I met

George Raft. He was a very nice guy and soon we were good pals. He was going round with a girl who was the star of *Show Boat* (the New York production), Helen Morgan, and sometimes she would come to our club (by the way, it was called the Avalon Club), and I would have my pianist play a very small piano on the dance floor, while Helen would sing some of the songs from her show accompanied by me on my trumpet. She used to sit on top of the piano. Naturally, she didn't get paid for this but just did it for the pleasure she got from singing.

Helen shared a flat with another girl from her show and, as George Raft knew Dorothea was out of town on tour with *Cocoanuts,* he asked me if I would like to have some breakfast with the girls at the flat when we finished. It seemed quite a good idea at the time. I accepted the invitation and it was so enjoyable that we made it a habit. It was certainly better than having to go to Child's Restaurant at around six in the morning to get a bite to eat before turning in. I thought this was a great idea because the new girl friend was a terrific looking girl, that is, it was a great idea until her real boy friend (I hadn't had the pleasure of meeting him, but he put this right), returned from Chicago and said he would blast me if I didn't make myself scarce. Well, I don't think I've ever been so scarce in my life! She was a very nice girl though, and I found out later she only went around with the choicest of gangsters! I remember Helen Morgan used to tell George Raft she thought he should try for films. He was a very good looking type and was one of the best dressers I had met, and it wasn't long after that he broke into pictures. During those days reporters from the Press would go round to the different clubs to see what was happening in cabaret and to pick up any tit-bits of news for their columns.

Two of them who used to come in quite often were the famous Walter Winchell and Ed Sullivan. That, of course, was long before Ed Sullivan had one of the biggest TV shows in the States. They both gave my band some nice reviews and on one occasion a girl reporter, who came in now and then, asked me to take her to a new operetta which was opening. She had Press tickets given her, so we went together and, after a very pleasant evening, the next day Winchell's column said it looked like a romance between this girl and myself. Although I appreciated the publicity, there was no truth in it, as I hardly knew the girl. The show we saw was *Countess Maritza*, and we both had a good laugh when she told me she was sure Winchell didn't know she was married.

While at the Avalon Club we played to some strange looking characters, some of them pretty rough, and one night an Italian-looking guy danced by the band and asked me to come to his table for a drink. I went over and he introduced me to a couple of his pals, forgetting the girls at the table. They were attractive in a rather over-dressed way – I mean, they had plenty of 'rocks' dripping from their necks and arms, and they were all calling this fellow who invited me to the table Al. This Al said I played 'his kind of music' and he said when I left the party: 'Here, kid, take this and buy your girl friend some flowers!' He pressed a one hundred dollar bill into my hand, which he did on several occasions after that. The head-waiter said that was the 'nice side' of him and it wasn't till after our first meeting I learnt that I'd made friends with the famous Al Capone! 'Legs' Diamond would also drop into the Club on occasion for a drink, and a fellow who became rather well known by the name Dillinger! During those days I met quite a number of those characters and it was hard to realize when talking to them that they were some of the toughest guys you could ever meet.

Many a night a very famous trumpet player by the name of Red Nichols would come into the Club to hear my band and he paid me the highest compliment by saying he came in especially to hear my type of playing. Coming from a player of his reputation, this was indeed a compliment, and we became real good friends. Of course, he was one of the top recording stars with his Five Pennies and the mere fact that he came in all by himself to hear me was very flattering. He invited me to one of his recording sessions, which I enjoyed very much.

Right round the corner from the Avalon Club on 54th Street was another famous club called Chez Lopez. The attraction was the big band of Vincent Lopez and it was one of the top bands of New York. He was known throughout the States for his broadcasts and he also started to come to our Club to listen to my band. One night he asked me if I would consider giving up my band to join him – strictly as a soloist. I didn't have to play in the brass section, just play my soft style on special choruses. That was one of the strangest offers I ever had, and it took quite a bit of doing to refuse, but I liked standing in front of my own band again. Vincent Lopez was famous as a pianist and every time I hear his theme song, *Nola*, I remember his offer.

Every once in a while a few men would walk into the Avalon Club and, just to let you know they were police on a raid, they would always keep their hats on while going from table to table smelling the glasses and cups (just in case they contained liquor instead of coffee). This night, which I still remember vividly, they came in and within a few minutes the owner asked everyone to leave as the Club had been closed. In a split second I was out of a job again! What to do next? So when a very well known band called the California Ramblers asked me to go with them on a tour of some of the Eastern States, I accepted. We played at several of the big Universities, including Harvard and Yale at their Prom dances. One of the members of the band was Adrian Rollini, who was famous for his playing of the bass saxophone. It was quite unusual for them to ask me to join them as they were strictly a swinging bunch of the finest musicians in the country. But they seemed to like my style and we had some great times together on the tour.

When we arrived back in New York I was wondering what to do next as the Ramblers split up after the tour. But I remembered that, while at the Sunset Inn with the Abe Lyman Band at Santa Monica, I met a terrific character who was in Hollywood to make a cowboy film and she was called Texas Guinan. Well, I don't think there will ever be another personality like Texas Guinan! She owned her own club in New York, so I went over to her place to pay her a visit. She invited me to have some food with her and to see her revue, a floor show which was famous throughout the world. In the show were several beautiful girls dancing, including Ruby Keeler. But Texas was the real attraction of the place. When she walked on to the dance floor she pulled the house down. What a personality! She was well known for her 'catch phrase' 'Give the Little Girl a Big Hand' each time any of the kids would do a 'speciality' in the cabaret, and Texas would make the 'out of towners' spend more money by kidding them into it. She was really the Queen of Broadway! After a few trips to the Club I became acquainted with Barbara, one of the girls in the show, and once again it was breakfast at about six o'clock in the morning. She and

Ruby Keeler were room mates and they lived across the bay in Hoboken, New Jersey. After breakfast each morning I would put them on the ferry. One morning Ruby told me she was going around with Al Jolson and there was a possibility they might marry. Which, of course, did happen later. She was a very nice girl and an excellent tap-dancer and was the main feature of the Texas Guinan show – that is, next to Texas. Quite often after the show Texas Guinan would pack some of the kids in the show into her car and she would drive all of us down to her flat in Greenwich Village. Generally her brother would be there and he was quite well known in the underworld. Texas would insist on cooking ham and eggs herself and we would wind up about ten o'clock in the morning. The kids all loved 'Tex' and she took wonderful care of them. If they were ever sick she saw that they needed nothing.

One night Texas told us she was going to take all of us on a party while her Club was being re-decorated. She took us to a club where Harry Richman was entertaining. Of course, I had seen him in many films but it wasn't like seeing him in person singing some of the songs he had made famous. He came over to our table and bought us drinks and made Texas Guinan get up on the floor and do a number. It was like a great big party.

Ruby Keeler, having said she might be marrying Al Jolson, asked her room mate and me if we would like to go to see him in the production he was starring in on Broadway. It was all arranged and, of course, I don't think it possible for anyone ever again to match the dynamic personality of Al Jolson on stage. But the performance never really began until the end, when the show had finished. The audience would never let him leave the stage until he would come out, sometimes sit in the foot-lights and sing their requests. I have seen him carry on for an hour or more until he was practically unable to sing. What a wonderful performer. Ruby took us back stage after the show and introduced us. He already knew Barbara and he asked me if I wasn't the boy he had heard at the Metropolitan Opera House at the Charity Performance playing my trumpet. This, of course, was very gratifying and I was happy he remembered. You see, I was still in my early twenties, and this kind of compliment coming from the great Al Jolson, for the second time, 'sent me' – I think that is the phrase now being used for such occasions.

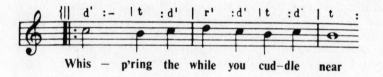

Whis — p'ring the while you cud–dle near

10. California Again

BY THIS TIME I had stayed in New York long enough to get my membership in the New York Musicians Union. Then one day I received a telegram from Hollywood. It was from Gus Arnheim (who was our pianist in the Abe Lyman band at the Sunset Inn in Santa Monica). He wanted me to join his new band at the Cocoanut Grove in the Ambassador Hotel, midway between Los Angeles and Hollywood. If I accepted I must fly at once! As I hadn't seen my mother and sister for a long while and in fact I hadn't been doing too well financially lately, I was really glad to have this offer. Gus made the proposition very worthwhile and, aside from my mother, I would be seeing some of that nice warm California sunshine again. I think by this time I had had enough travelling for the time being. I told all my friends in New York 'good-bye' and was on my way back home.

The first thing I did was to get a nice apartment just across the street from the hotel for my mother and me. She'd had such a hard life I thought the least I could do would be to let her get away from our house which still kept her too busy doing the housework. Being as tidy as she always was, I was pleased when I saw how happy she was in our new abode. Sometimes some of the boys in the band would visit us and Mama enjoyed making them a meal. They, in return, liked her a lot, so her life was much more happy than it had been while I was away in New York.

This was in 1927, and the band's opening at the Grove was sensational. Almost overnight our broadcasts put us right on top of the ladder (we broadcast every night from about 10.30 to midnight), and during an interval Gus Arnheim and I would go up into a small room in the hotel and I would broadcast request solos on my trumpet. I have never seen so many motion-picture stars in any one room I played in. It seemed everyone connected with pictures came there to see or be seen. Gus Arnheim had found a new singer for the band who made a big reputation for himself within a short time. His name was Russ Columbo.

Some of America's finest musicians were assembled for this band and I was very happy working with Ray Lopez, my former 'side-kick' in the Abe Lyman Orchestra. Ray by this time had learned to read music a little, which was most necessary for the arrangements we were playing, but what he lacked in reading was certainly made up for with his terrific cornet playing. I believe I explained before that in those quite early days of the big band, Ray was to me the greatest. He came from the South and played just as they did there, and if you closed your eyes you would swear he was coloured – just about the highest compliment I can pay him. I had a wonderful time while with that band and met many, many interesting people in the Grove.

At that time all the most beautiful girls in the world were coming to Hollywood to try and break into films. Even then Hollywood was comparatively small and when a new face appeared in the Cocoanut Grove the boys in the band were the first to know. I remember it well because the most lovely looking girl was dancing with a friend of mine, who was the son of a wealthy car-dealer. I was rather anxious to learn more about this girl and when I went to Tommy's table, he introduced me to her. He said her name was Lucille Le Seur. She was really terrific! She was about twenty years old and she had a wonderful warm personality. Tommy started bringing her into the Grove several nights a week, and one night he told me Lucille had decided to change her name, as she was going to try for pictures and she thought 'Joan Crawford' might be more suitable. She won a local talent contest when she was thirteen, danced on the Broadway stage, and later in films she starred in *Forsaking All Others, A Woman's Face* and *Whatever Happened to Baby Jane?* She has had fifty years of stardom.

A short while later I was invited to Joan's twenty first birthday party in her home in Beverly Hills. It was a lovely little bungalow and when I arrived it was already late as I had to finish work before I could go along to the party. I like to recall that Joan answered the door herself and how beautiful she looked in the dress she was wearing. She could really wear clothes. I think she even looked better than at anytime I had seen her while dancing to our music. For me the evening got off to a good start when she threw her arms around me and placed a great big unforgettable kiss right on my lips! Boy! What a girl! What a lucky guy Tommy was to have her for his girl-friend. I tried my best not to respond too heartily to her loving embrace as Tommy was standing not too far away, watching the moment I shall never forget. Joan grabbed me by the hand and ushered me inside where I met some big movie names and it was only just before I had arrived that they had asked her to do the 'Charleston'. She had made a big reputation as a 'Charleston Dancer' before coming to Hollywood and being a good sport she did a most exciting dance and then she got everybody to join in and try it – offering a bottle of champagne to the winner of the Great Charleston Contest. I'm sure no one at the party could ever imagine this beautiful dancing girl becoming one of the foremost stars of the film world. Not long after that she was doing her first part in a picture that was to pave the way for the journey which would lead to success, glamour, riches, and a lot of good acting thrown in. And believe me when I say it couldn't have happened to a nicer person.

At this point I would just like to add that this party, like so many of the parties I went to in Hollywood frequented by the top film stars, was unlike the usual press stories you could read almost any day about the 'wild goings-on'. I honestly did not see one person who put a foot wrong. That was usually the case, but it didn't make good 'copy' for the columnists.

Someone else who was just starting out in the picture business at the same time was Loretta Young. She used to come to the Grove quite often and when the band had a break we would generally go out on to the large terrace running around the Ambassador Hotel and sit in the wonderful warm night air. Loretta and some of the other kids would always join us and it was like having a party. The musicians in the band were a good class type of boy – all fairly young and they mixed with the people who came to dance to our music. Most of them were college boys and the girls seemed to find them attractive, rather like a big happy family. Loretta Young had some sisters and they were all beautiful. They lived in a large house near the hotel and I was invited over there a few times with some of the rest of the guys. Sally, one of her sisters, was in pictures too and made quite a name before Loretta got started. They were really nice girls.

Every Wednesday night was Movie Night at the Cocoanut Grove. You couldn't even get near the place unless you booked well in advance or had the 'necessary' to make the head-waiter realize that the night couldn't be a success unless he found you a table. Movie Night meant that most of the stars would come to the Grove, including the top producers and directors, in fact just everybody in show business, and during the evening many of the stars who could do an act would be called upon to come on to the floor and entertain.

A very similar thing to that had started at The Sunset Inn in Santa Monica. Everyone from opera stars to knock-about comedians would do their stuff in a show that lasted for a couple of hours sometimes. Of course, it would have been impossible to begin to pay these people what they ordinarily would have charged for this public appearance, but they all happily joined in the fun and really 'let their hair down'. What wonderful nights they were! Many a time Eddie Cantor would pull the place apart when he sang *Dinah*.

One night when I was playing a solo spot in the band, I noticed a fellow and a girl dancing right in front of me who were listening intently. When I finished playing the man said to me: 'Pardon me, but you play the trumpet very beautifully, so softly, just like a whisper. It sounds more like a violin than a horn.' I thanked him and appreciated his tribute and when he had danced on his way Gus Arnheim asked me if I knew who the guy was and I had to admit I didn't. Then Gus told me it was the world famous Heifitz! Well, this made quite an impression on me and I began to think – 'Just a whisper – *huh* – a whisper?' As I mentioned earlier my friend Johnny Schonberger had written a tune a few years back called *Whispering* so I decided why not call mine the 'Whispering Trumpet'? Yes, that's how I got the idea through Heifitz and it eventually led me to using *Whispering* as my signature tune. Since I had been playing in night-clubs, starting at The Sunset Inn, I used to take our guitarist with me and play very quietly for people sitting at the tables during a break in the dance music. I got quite a reputation doing this and before long I was asked to play on movie sets with, maybe, an organ or just a guitar so that the stars would have what was known as 'atmosphere' music. This was, of course, in the silent days and, aside from the extra money I made, it was interesting.

I had a very good friend, Frank Borzage, who was probably the highest rated film director in Hollywood at the time, and he was directing Janet Gaynor and Charles Farrell in their pictures. Frank Borzage began acting as a teenager and became a full time film director at the very early age of twenty-four. Each time he did a film with them he would want me on the set to play 'side-line' music. One of the films he directed with Janet and Charlie was *Seventh Heaven*, and I remember that during a scene where Janet had stolen a loaf of bread, I had to play *Love Here is my Heart*, which was the favourite piece of music of both of them. It would make Janet cry during the scene, and it helped them get into the mood for their love scene. Another film they did together was *The Street Angel* for which I did the same kind of thing.

One morning when I was having breakfast at the corner drug store, I walked into the street and I saw a young girl taking a look at the motor of her car. Not wanting to leave a lady in distress, I asked her if I could be of help. She said, 'I hope so' and, although I didn't know the front end of a car from the rear, I immediately started touching wires and things and looked as if I knew what I was doing, and quite by chance, when I asked her to step on the starter, the engine actually started. I'm sure I was much more surprised than she. I still don't know what was wrong with it, but anyway I was to her a hero. I thought it may be impolite not to ask her name. She said Sue Carroll and little did I know then that at a later date I would be directing the music in a film she was to star in. That was even before she married Alan Ladd.

This was all happening while I was still at the Cocoanut Grove and, as I said earlier, Sam Warner and I were on the way to a party at Marie Prevost's house in Beverly Hills, when he told me that he and his brother Jack Warner were working on an idea that would make pictures talk. He explained the general idea to me and, of course, it all sounded too far fetched. But he had great confidence in it, and sure enough in October 1927 the first talking picture opened in New York. It was, as you probably know, called *The Jazz Singer,* and starred Al Jolson. I went to the opening of that film in Hollywood.

Naturally, before the film went on, the audience didn't know just what to expect. We knew the actors would be heard speaking their lines and singing their songs, but how was it going to sound? What would it be like? Would this new medium take over from the live theatre? There was great expectancy! The entire cinema was buzzing with excitement! Well, at last the house lights started to dim and there was an uncommon hush. The curtains opened to the terrific music of the first talking picture! I still remember the thrill of it all, and I don't ever expect to hear such applause again as was given to Al Jolson when he sang *Sonny Boy*. I got the impression that the audience thought they were hearing him 'live' in the theatre. The experience was really uncanny. Then I knew just what Sam Warner had been talking about when he told me about his movies that would talk. What a tragedy Sam couldn't have been there. You see, Sam died of pneumonia the day before the film opened in New York. Just a day too soon!

I became acquainted with a fellow who was a writer of short stories for 'pulp' magazines and we were going around with two girls who were living out in the valley – out past the Warner Brothers' First National Studios in Burbank. Our girl friends were living with two other girls in a large house and we used to go out to see them together; and one night this writer told me he had written a scenario for a film (that's what they called scripts then) and Jack Warner had asked him to bring it to the studio the next day so that he could take a look at it. This was a big break for my friend and naturally he was excited. The outcome was, Jack Warner liked the story and bought it and that was just the beginning of the long and colourful career of Darryl Zanuck! He later became Head of Production for Warner Brother Pictures on his way to attaining heights in the motion picture industry second to none, as well as being President of Twentieth-Century-Fox.

Lots of interesting things happened to me while at the Cocoanut Grove. One was meeting a really lovely young American-Indian girl. She wasn't very tall but what there was of her was first class. She was so beautiful everyone would look at her on account of her appearance. On my birthday Gus Arnheim let me take the night off and I took this girl dancing. Where to? The Cocoanut Grove, of course! I felt as though I was out with one of the top movie stars – everyone's eyes were on the girl I was dancing with. One of the big producers came to our table and asked if she would like to come to his studio for a film test. Of course, I could understand him making this request, as she had the most wonderful great big black eyes, and soft skin which was slightly tan, or maybe red, being Indian – American Indian. She declined his offer and this I couldn't believe. That was the only reason every girl was in Hollywood. But she just wasn't interested. When I took her home after a wonderful night I asked her why she had refused the offer of a possible chance to become someone big in pictures. She told me she had to get back home to her family as they had found more oil on her land, and I later learned that she came from one of the wealthiest Indian families. But it was a marvellous birthday and I was more than sorry she couldn't stay.

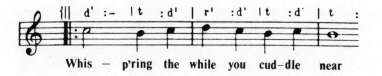

Whis — p'ring the while you cud-dle near

11. Marriage

'WELL,' YOU MIGHT ask, 'but what about Dorothea?' A fellow had to go out now and then with a girl, especially when it was his birthday. At that time anyway, Dorothea was in New York, or at least I thought she was, until the very next day when the telephone rang and as I lifted the receiver a lovely voice said, 'Hello!' and, of course, I knew it was Dorothea. I thought she was speaking from New York as I had spoken to her quite often since being back in Los Angeles. When she asked me how I would like to come down to see her at the Biltmore Hotel, I asked her what she meant and she explained she had been asked by a famous dress designer if she would come to Los Angeles to show the 'line' – and here she was! She wanted it to be a surprise.

The outcome of our meeting at the Biltmore was that I talked her into remaining in Los Angeles so that we could be married. She met my mother. Mama was rather sad, as most mothers are when they realize their 'little boy' is about to be married. She liked Dorothea though and thought she was a lovely girl, which made me very pleased. Dorothea was very sweet to her and I

121

felt lucky that they were hitting it off together so well.

As soon as Dorothea had completed her job with the dress designer we were wed and Gus Arnheim was my best man. The boys in the band threw a big party for me on the night before and we had a very merry time. I felt that, inasmuch as I was to be a married man, I should swear off attending the poker parties we . indulged in each Saturday night. And I stuck to my word for about two weeks.

The one thing I didn't care for about getting married was that my mother would not hear of living with us, so she took up residence at our house again and this meant her being alone, with the exception of the times when my sister Vera came to visit her. Vera and Harvey had moved back to Los Angeles and had luckily bought a house near Mama. At least they would be together part of the time. But I knew my mother would miss me.

Dorothea and I took another apartment in Hollywood and it was great fun fixing it up with little things we bought. I braved her cooking and tried to make her think it was a lot better than it was in the beginning, and sometimes I would bring home a bottle of wine to go with the sumptuous feast she had prepared. This always seemed to make her unnaturally gay, but then as time went on, instead of getting gay after a drink or two, she began to start resenting little things I did. I realized she was only eighteen and probably couldn't drink even the small amount we had on hand. And certainly I wasn't leading her on as I was practically a teetotaller. I liked maybe one cocktail before dinner – maybe not that – and I was perfectly satisfied if I indulged in a glass of wine with the meal. But Dorothea began to ask me to bring whisky or gin home as she enjoyed a drink on occasion. This seemed nothing out of the ordinary, and I would bring in a bottle now and then. Just a little something to have on hand in case guests came in. But I soon realized that although we did not have that many friends coming over, the bottles were emptying faster than usual. And sometimes when I came home she would be in a sulky mood. Her eyes wouldn't look straight at me – almost avoiding mine. I was getting a worried feeling about this and it became more and more easy to start a quarrel.

That's the last thing I wanted to happen, but it was difficult to avoid. I tried to say I had forgotten to bring anything home to drink, which infuriated her and she could easily make things unpleasant. I was very much in love with her and I thought if I gave in a little maybe she would be happy. This I tried and I was right. She did get happier, but tighter at the same time. The situation became more clear with every week that passed, and I began to wonder how this could happen to one of the most wonderful girls I had ever met.

Sometimes when I brought friends home with me she would be as charming as anyone could possibly be. Then she would leave the room for a few moments and when she joined us again I would notice she was a little the worse for wear. How could that be? Maybe we hadn't had a drink at all with my friends, but she certainly was getting 'high', and I did not know how. I thought it may be wise to try to find out and it didn't take me long to discover the source of her hilarity at one moment and her nasty little snide remarks the next. A hidden bottle in the clothes hamper! This just couldn't happen to a girl like Dorothea! It just couldn't!

Once in a while I came in and she would be waiting for me, proud of the nice dinner she had prepared, and a guy could never wish for a more wonderful wife. And her cooking was improving all the time. We'd have a lot of fun together and I knew she was trying hard to avoid the temptation of just one little one. I knew she was very much in love with me and I also realized I wasn't much of a match for that bottle, which may be hidden in all sorts of places.

It was heart breaking when she really felt sorry, to hear her cry because she had hurt me, and I always prayed she would remain sorry and try and overcome her terrible problem. Sometimes she hated herself for what was happening to us and would bring me a bottle from its hiding place to dispose of, to lessen the temptation. I was so thankful the first few times she swore she would give it up, but each time I was more and more disappointed. I would leave her after having a nice dinner and when I came home after work one would never know it was the same person.

What could I possibly do to help her? Maybe if I put my foot down and wasn't so forgiving it might help. The first time I told her that if she did not stop drinking I would call it quits and that would be the end of everything. Whereupon she went into the bedroom and I wondered why she was staying in there so long, and the answer was she had swallowed a bottle of iodine, and it was only through the speed of the ambulance and the doctor's care that she didn't accomplish what she had set out to do. And was I scared? How could I be so lousy when I realized I was responsible? I really had only wanted to frighten her, hoping it would help her overcome her desires. Then, for a short time at least, she did her very best to forget drinking and we were very happy together. I was so thankful I bought her a beautiful dog, thinking it might help her pass the lonely hours while I was playing at night at the Grove.

One evening after one of my broadcasts I was called

to the telephone and I was asked if I could come to the Montmartre Cafe on Hollywood Boulevard the next day to meet Eddie Brandstetter, the proprietor of that famous restaurant. I naturally wondered what it was all about, but kept the appointment. Somewhat to my surprise Eddie asked me if I would like to form my own band again and play at the Montmartre. Strangely enough, this required a bit of thought as Gus Arnheim and I got on very well together and he had treated me so well while I was with the band, it was hard to think of leaving him. But after due consideration (and the idea that I had always liked having my own band) I finally accepted. It was terribly difficult telling Gus I wanted to leave, but he understood and wished me well.

I got a very good bunch of boys together and opened at this glamorous spot in the heart of Hollywood. I had a nightly broadcast from ten till twelve over the Warner Brothers Radio Station. The relief band was a small tango orchestra, led by a very fine violinist by the name of Xavier Cugat. When I say relief band I mean that while my band took a rest Cugat would play in the meantime – twice during the night. Here again, the movie crowd would assemble and it was a show-place where tourists and people from everywhere would come to see the stars. The Montmartre was just half a block from the world famous Grauman's Chinese Theatre which was also on Hollywood Boulevard. Radio was still so young that each evening during our broadcasts people could telephone their requests and we would play them; especially the movie crowd would 'phone, knowing their names would be announced over the air.

During this time Dorothea unfortunately became ever a greater source of worry to me as she was in the difficult position of being alone so much of the time. When she was alone with Fu, our dog, she would drink to cheer herself up a bit and if she was out with friends, she would drink to be sociable and, of course, there was only one outcome in either case – blind drunk. The habit had really set in and, although she would cry on occasion when she felt sorry and repentant, even that was beginning to get less and less. Dorothea was turning into a person I did not know. Sometimes our quarrels would last most of the night and she thought nothing of breaking the nearest thing she could lay her hands on. I resorted to everything I knew and at last her mother came from New York to stay with us for a short time when she heard what was happening. She thought she might help put things right but the best she got out of her trip was a broken heart. She even went as far as to tell me the best thing I could do was to leave Dorothea, because she could see no hope of any happiness in the future. She confided that Dorothea's father had died a drunkard.

There were now only a few hours a day when she was anything near her real self and I knew my love for her was turning to pity. But I was positive in my own mind that if Dorothea surmised that I would really leave her, she would not hesitate to resort to the iodine again. Her mother, who was a wonderful woman, assured me it was the only way out, so I tried just once more to frighten her with this threat and sure enough – iodine! By this time my friends were advising what they would do, but when you are faced with a problem of this nature it isn't all that easy to overcome, no matter which way you try. And the worst part was I was beginning to dislike her for much of the time, but not enough really to take the step that would free me of all the unhappiness; but if I did, what would happen to her? And so it would go on day after day.

My band by this time was really popular with the

movie crowd at parties given at their homes, where we would go after finishing at the Montmartre. Frequently I would be asked by William Randolph Hearst, the well-known newspaper publisher in the States, to bring my band down to Malibu Beach where Marion Davies, the film star, had a most beautiful Beach house, and play for breakfast in the large kitchen for just a few guests. The parties were really something. Aside from swimming in the large pool in front of the house, between the house and the sea, the stars would all join in playing kids' games, and they all had a wonderful time. It was strange to see those people enjoying themselves in such a simple way and having so much fun. The party would break up at times for them to get to the studio to be made-up for that day's shooting.

My band did this quite often and I started getting so many calls to play at different parties that I finally had to limit our appearances for we could have killed ourselves playing at the Montmartre, then all night after we finished work. All this time the band would very often be playing at the film studios during the day where there was a night club set and they required a dance band. I suppose we played in dozens of pictures at Metro-Goldwyn-Mayer, Paramount, First National and many of the other studios.

1. *Above:* Me playing trumpet with the Gus Arnheim band at the Cocoanut Grove, Hollywood, 1927

2. *Below:* At the fashionable Monseigneur Night Club, London, 1931

3. *Above:* Our instrumental line-up at the Monseigneur Night Club, 1931

4. *Below:* Our 'gang' at the Cafe Anglais, Leicester Square, London, 1932

5. *Above:* The Mack Sennett Bathing Beauties with Ben Turpin on the sand at Santa Monica during filming. Note pier in background where my mother and I often fished.

6. *Below:* Agora Cinema, Brussels, 1932. What a thrill it was shaking hands with King Albert of Belgium. I still remember my knees shaking!

7.   *Above:* The Belgian Royal
Family at the Royal Com-
mand Performance, 1932

8.   *Below:* Jean Harlow with Ben
Lyon in *Hell's Angels,* 1928

9. *Above:* 'The Cubs' with me at the Kit-Kat Club, London, 1933

10. *Below:* Dorothea . . . if only she could have remained like this . . .

11. *Above:* After our first meeting i
didn't take Joan Crawford long t
make it in pictures in a big way. Stil
from *Our Dancing Daughters*

12. *Left:* My favourite picture of Jea
Harlow taken during our romanc

13. *Left:* With singer Peggy Dell at the Kit-Kat, 1933

14. *Below:* My good friend Ford Sterling with the Keystone Cops

15. *Above:* Duke Ellington at the start of our friendship which I shall always treasure

16. *Below:* Sophie Tucker was one of the first stars I worked with in the early days . . . and one of the greatest!

17. *Above:* Pinfire, my racehorse. Thanks to Tommy Weston, Harry Wragg, Michael Carr and some of the others, he didn't do too badly!

18. *Below:* The Paul Whiteman 'Rhythm Boys' Bing Crosby, Al Rinker and Harry Baris while working with my band at the Montmartre Cafe.

19. *Above:* A bit of relaxation with some of my greyhounds at Wembley Stadium

20. *Left:* Denny Dennis . . . from an electrician to one of the all-time greats among British dance-band vocalists

21. *Below:* Louis Armstrong . . . a guy I like to remember for the good times we had together

22. *Above:* Palace Ballroom, Douglas, Isle of Man on TT night . . . over ten thousand dancers!

23. *Below:* Al Bowlly . . . one of the pioneer 'crooners'

24. *Above:* Kay Kimber ... chosen most beautiful newcomer to Hollywood for her part in *Dodsworth* with Walter Huston. A production photograph from *High Button Shoes*, Hippodrome Theatre, London

25. *Above:* A totally unique photograph of some of the leading band-leaders of their day in their roles as instrumentalists: Back row violinists (*l to r*) Bert Ambrose, Joe Loss, Maurice Winnick, Sydney Lipton. Front row (*l to r*) Roy Fox (trumpet), Harry Roy (clarinet), Billy Ternent (saxophone). Pianist in forefront Lew Stone

26. *Below:* With Geraldo (left) and Henry Hall

27. *Above:* A youthful Frank
Sinatra when we met in Glasgow at the Empire Theatre

28. *Above:* Eileen O'Donnell . . .
brought a great deal of happiness into my life

29. *Below:* One of the nicest
things to happen to me during my lifetime . . . Gary, my
son

30. *Left:* Me today

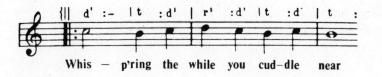

Whis — p'ring the while you cud–dle near

12. Jean Harlow

ONCE I WAS asked to take the band to the William Fox Studios and we arrived very early that morning on the set. When we got there, the extras were already waiting for the director to start the proceedings and I got up on the bandstand and looked down at the ringside table at ⎯ of the most terrific girls I'd ever seen. I knew ⎯ctically every film extra in Hollywood (we met them so often in different films), but I certainly had never seen this girl before. I must explain that in those early Hollywood days it didn't seem to make much difference how long the director took to finish a picture; so while they were lighting the set, or setting up for the next scene, my band would play and the director would grab one of the girls and everyone had a dance, just to pass the time.

That morning after seeing this new girl I smiled at her and quietly asked her if she would like to dance. She smiled back and nodded yes, so I introduced myself. There were four ladies at the table, one of them her mother, a lovely looking woman, strictly society. I couldn't wait to get this girl on to the dance floor. I didn't know whether her hair was blonde or silver, or what colour you would call it. I had never seen hair like that. Although all the extra girls were out of this world, she stood out like a million! Well, we started dancing and I told her I knew she must be new in Hollywood and she wondered how I knew. I said that if she had been there long I would have been the very first to know. She explained she had just arrived from Chicago and wanted to try to break into pictures; her mother had come along with her that morning to keep her company. I asked her name and she said it was Harlean Carpenter, but she was going to change it because if her grandfather in Chicago heard she was in Hollywood trying to get into films he would disinherit her. So she had four different names she was considering and mentioned them to me. The one I told her I liked best was Jean Harlow. She said: 'You really like it?' I said I thought it suited her and she said: 'That's it, you have made up my mind for me – Jean Harlow it is!' From that moment she was known by the name I helped her to select. Then I asked her if I could telephone her. Her answer was in the affirmative and that same evening I 'phoned her at the small house she had purchased in Beverly Hills and invited her to come down to see me at the Montmartre that night. She said she would get into the car and drive by to see me, which she did. When my band got a break I asked Xavier Cugat to prolong his playing time for a bit, as I had some important business to take care of – and that night was the start of Jean and I meeting at the Montmartre nearly every night for a year. She would drive in to see me and we would sit in the auto-park next to the Montmartre, listening to Cugat's music coming out through the open window.

One night a few weeks later, Jean came to the Club to meet me as usual and she was so excited I asked her

what it was all about. She said that a man had stopped
her on Hollywood Boulevard while she was shopping
and asked her if she would like to come to the Hal
Roach Studios to see about getting a part in a film they
were making. She asked me if I would drive her out
there in my car for the audition the next day. Of course
I was happy to. The Studio was in Culver City, very
close to MGM. I waited for her while she went into the
Studio and when she came out I could see at once that
she had been successful! It was for just a small part in
a Laurel and Hardy comedy *Double Whoopie* but she was
so thrilled and I was, of course, very happy for her.
When the picture was previewed at a small picture
house in Hollywood, I took her to see it and I have
never seen anybody so excited. As I said, it was only a
tiny part but she felt like a star. She looked great on the
screen though.

You may remember the scene. In it Jean entered the
lobby of the hotel, then walked over to the elevator and
entered it. A few moments later the elevator doors
opened again and she started to walk out. But as the
doors closed behind her her skirt was caught, pulling
the backside off and exposing her brief panties as she
walked away from the camera.

Aside from meeting Jean each evening, we still met
on film sets during the day, sometimes when she was
still doing 'extra' work and she seemed to get more
beautiful all the time. Then, one night she got out of
her car in the auto-park and ran over to me. She had
been stopped again in the street and was asked to come
to MGM Studios for a screen test for a picture they
were going to make. I drove her out to Culver City
again, this time waiting for about three hours outside
the Studio, and when she came out she was again very
excited. I asked her how she thought she had done and

she said she didn't know but thought they liked her. She said a very nice actor named Ben Lyon had read the part in the scene with her, and he was most helpful. She said she thought the producer's name was Howard Hughes. He was very rich and had told her the film was to be about aeroplanes; so that was the way Jean Harlow got her first starring part in *Hell's Angels.*

It was some time before she started on the film and in the meantime we continued seeing a lot of each other. One evening at the Montmartre I was asked to go to the table of a young fellow who was sitting all alone and he invited me to sit down. He said: 'I understand you have been seeing a great deal of my wife!' For a moment I was stunned. I knew that Jean *had* been married, but had separated from her husband who lived in Chicago. But not separated enough, as far as I was concerned when I heard this! In a nice quiet manner he took a pistol from his pocket and let me take a good look at it, telling me at the same time that if I didn't stop seeing her, he'd do more than just show it to me. He said he had made the trip all the way from Chicago just to deliver this message to me and, naturally, I explained I knew Jean had been married but that she assured me it was all off. Inasmuch as I didn't relish going around dead, he was a very nice guy and agreed that he should meet Jean again and settle everything one way or the other. I meanwhile agreed not to see her until they decided the outcome, which only took a few days; then Jean 'phoned to tell me he had gone back to Chicago. This was some of the most interesting news I had heard for many a day.

What was happening to me? Here I was falling madly in love with Jean when I knew I didn't have the right to. I also realized she was very much in love with me and that if I were free we would marry. We talked about it a lot, but there was always Dorothea. How could I do this to her? No telling what might happen to her, and I made myself believe that, if she had been with someone who could be with her every night so that she wouldn't have so much time on her own, especially if they had a few drinks together, maybe she would be different. But the fact that I didn't drink all that much and was away from her nearly every night – I just did not know the answer. Jean, of course, knew my predicament and was understanding about the whole thing. She couldn't have been sweeter. So we continued to see one another hoping some miracle would put things right.

As I mentioned before, the Montmartre was just a stone's throw from Grauman's Chinese Theatre on Hollywood Boulevard, which was probably the most famous cinema in the world. You have probably heard how each time there was a premiere of a new film, the stars would always leave their hand and foot prints in the wet concrete in the courtyard in front of the theatre. One of the opening nights I remember well was the first showing of *Broadway Melody*. Arthur Freed and Nacio Herb Brown, who wrote the songs, had previously come to see me to give me an orchestration of the score. After the opening all the stars from the film came in to dance to my music and, of course, we were the very first dance band to play all the music from the picture. It's still nice to think every time I hear *I'm Singing in the Rain* – I introduced it!

During that year, hotel managements started bringing out big name bands from the East, and right across the street from the Montmartre was the large new Hotel Roosevelt which was about to open and they engaged the New York band of George Olsen. George's music was well known on records and we became quite good friends. He stayed at the hotel for some time, then Irving Aaronson and his Commanders were brought out from Chicago and Irving made a great hit with his orchestra. He had a wonderful entertaining band and while they played, the crowd of dancers gathered round on the dance floor to listen. Irving became one of my very best pals and we used to play a lot of golf together – a really nice guy.

It was just about this time that Paul Whiteman brought his orchestra out to Hollywood to make a film called *The King of Jazz,* and he used to come in to hear my band and spend the evening dancing. By then his music had gone from strength to strength and I had always been one of his greatest admirers. In my estimation, Paul Whiteman did more for dance music than any other person I knew. Everything he did was BIG! Even when he had opened with his first dance orchestra at the Alexandria Hotel in Los Angeles (I told you earlier about hearing him that night), his orchestrations were big – in advance of anything we had been hearing. He always had great vocal talent and when he told me one night the film had broken down I immediately· told the boss about it and suggested he get the Paul Whiteman Rhythm Boys to appear in cabaret at the Montmartre. This he did, and that was how I first met Bing Crosby, Harry Baris and Al Rinker. They were an instant hit in our floor show and I'll always remember the way they sang *Mississippi Mud.*

Bing Crosby was an outstanding figure in the big band era of Paul Whiteman and after his film debut in *King of Jazz,* his musical comedies included *The Road to Singapore, White Christmas* and *High Society.* But at that time Bing didn't have quite as much money as he has now, so I used to take the boys out to movie parties after work and we would play and sing all night till about five or six o'clock, and Bing, Harry and Al were mighty pleased to make one hundred and fifty dollars, about thirty pounds then, split between them which helped the weekly budget. I remember one night we played at Tom Mix's house in Beverly Hills and there were the usual stars present who, of course, thought the Rhythm Boys were great. They were something quite new and all had terrific personalities. They were liked wherever we went. And Charlie Chaplin (not to be outdone) played the fiddle.

One day I was at MGM Studios where I had been invited by Lionel Barrymore to watch him direct a film which was quite an unusual thing for him to do. He had been in films since 1920 and played many of his later roles in a wheel chair – in the *Dr Kildare* series as Doctor Gillespie. He was the eldest of the family, Edith was next and John had the greatest talent. Of course, Lionel was always busy acting, but on this occasion he had agreed to direct this picture by way of a change. I think it is the ambition of a lot of actors to direct at some time or other and I think Barrymore was an excellent director on account of his outstanding acting ability. While watching him, a very good friend of mine came on the set to see Barrymore, and she was surprised to see me sitting there. It was Carole Lombard. She watched for a while and then asked me if I would like to come to her dressing room for a cup of tea, which I did. She was a most marvellous girl – you would never know she was one of the top stars. I think she and Joan Crawford were two of the nicest people in Hollywood. I stayed with her until she had to go back to her set, so she walked with me to the gate where she introduced me to Clark Gable, then I said 'goodbye'.

One of my very best friends in Hollywood was Noah Beery, one of the real 'tough guys', at least in the parts he played; but away from pictures he was one of the most gentle people I have ever met. Although he was tall and heavily built, like his brother, Wallace Beery, he spoke very softly all the time. He was a great out-of-doors man. He always had bear meat and venison stacked away in the large ice box at the Montmartre, and he talked me into having some bear meat one evening when he was in, but I would prefer a good old steak anytime. Noah owned a beautiful Trout Club up in the mountains about a three hour drive from Hollywood. The hotel part was built right on a stream, and this was surrounded by log cabins. The hotel was built of logs also. The idea was you could drive there to do a bit of fishing, knowing you wouldn't be disappointed, as the stream was 'stocked' with trout which were raised nearby. Noah had a marvellous bass voice and he liked it when I took my trumpet with me so he could sing and I could play. This we would do late at night after everyone had turned in, right in front of the biggest fireplace I have ever seen. Great large logs burning; one of my most pleasant memories, and what a wonderful guy!

One warm beautiful night, we decided to have a 'weenie'. bake on top of a nearby mountain. It wasn't very high but it still had to be reached on horseback. By the way, 'weenie' is what 'hot-dogs' were called at the time. The very thought of my getting on a horse to ride up a mountain trail filled me with a certain amount of trembling. My experience on a flying steed was exactly nil and, although I wanted to go on this moonlight ride, I was still scared stiff. Noah knew this and very kindly gave me an animal which was extremely quiet (Noah said so), and at the same time rather lazy. This sounded quite a combination to me, as I had no intention of becoming a bronco-buster, then or at any other time. I was fitted out with some cowboy gear and we started on our way. Noah suggested I stay in the rear of the other riders so that the horse would just follow on after them, but the horse had different ideas about the whole thing. When we came to a little path which ordinarily led back to the club my horse turned into it and continued on until I nearly pulled my arms off trying to stop him. Then back I went to the starting point and tried it again with the same success I had just encountered. This horse was truly lazy, just like Noah said, so much so he had obviously decided he would prefer being in bed than on the trail climbing a steep mountain. As Noah had also told me, this animal was really quiet about the whole thing – very quiet and determined! Do you think I could get him to change his mind? Not a bit of it! Anyway, by this time the gang must have been half way to those beautiful sizzling hot-dogs, not realizing I was still trying to get Lonely (how could I forget his name?) past that homeward path back to the stables. Lonely was the operative word as far as I was concerned. I had the entire place to myself until one of the 'guides' came back to see what had happened to me. He told me what I had done wrong in my endeavour to play cowboy, but I was sure Lonely was fast asleep by this time. Probably the only 'fast' thing he ever did in his life.

By this time Jean Harlow had started working on *Hell's Angels* and on account of having to be on the set so early, she couldn't drive down to see me as often as she had been doing. So our meetings were mostly weekends at her house in Beverly Hills. Many a time I would help her read her lines after dinner for the next day's shooting. She was an excellent cook! She really worked hard to try to become an actress, as she had practically no acting experience before this terrific break came her way. But she *had* to act looking like she did! Never have I seen a more beautiful figure, greener eyes, or a lovelier pink and white complexion. I can truthfully say that, although for some reason or other she became associated with a certain amount of scandal later, she was really one of the nicest girls I have ever met.

One night while I was still playing at the Montmartre Cafe, a very lovely looking girl and an elderly man were dancing together and stayed right in front of me while I was playing. They both kept watching, especially when I played one of my 'whispering' trumpet solos and when we had finished and took a break, the gentleman asked me to come to his table. I went over and he introduced himself as Florenz Ziegfeld and the beautiful girl he was with as Marilyn Miller. Naturally I knew I was talking to the great Ziegfeld, of Ziegfeld Follies fame, the man who staged the Follies in Palm Beach, Florida, which I had seen when Peggy Prevost was in it; and Marilyn Miller was one of Broadway's brightest stars.

They invited me to sit down and Ziegfeld asked me how I would like to conduct some of the music on the film Marilyn was going to make at the Warner Brothers First National Studios. He said the picture was going to be called *Sally* after the New York hit Marilyn had starred in and, as she sang some songs in it, she wanted me to accompany her on my trumpet. Primarily she was a great dancer and, as her voice wasn't as good as her dancing, she said I must join her. Ziegfeld told me he would like me to bring my band and augment it with the studio musicians, making a total of almost thirty in the orchestra. I was really taken aback at this suggestion, but we arranged a deal and sure enough when I went out to the studios in the valley in North Hollywood to start rehearsing the orchestra, I found the added studio musicians were all from Los Angeles Symphony Orchestra. One of the trumpet players was the finest trumpet teacher in Los Angeles and you can imagine my feelings when I saw the rest of them – some of the leading players in the country – especially when I had always stood in front of my own dance band and had never conducted a large orchestra like this. I'm sure most of the musicians knew more about it than I did, but we got through the rehearsal without mishap and Marilyn Miller couldn't have been nicer.

Ziegfeld was at the rehearsal one day and said he thought it was going along very well. Then came the day when we went on the actual set to film the sequence I was to be used on. Marilyn was to sing one of the most famous songs from the show called *Look for The Silver Lining* and what made it most difficult for me was the fact that she was several yards away from me and I had to use earphones for the first time, while the orchestra was quite a long way from me in the other direction. These days, of course, that wouldn't mean a thing, as the whole thing would probably be 'dubbed' in, but that day it was, to say the least, quite an experience. After we had finished, Marilyn came over and thanked me with a very nice kiss on the cheek, which made it all worthwhile. Also in that scene was a friend of mine who, I'm sure, you have seen many times in some of his earlier comedies – Ford Sterling of the Keystone Cops.

Just about this same time a well-known singer and recording star called Nick Lucas had sung a song in a picture which is still popular today, and he was to record it, so he asked me to accompany him with my trumpet. He played the guitar and we went to the new Brunswick recording studios in Los Angeles and recorded *Tip Toe Through The Tulips*.

I used to do the same thing with a girl called June Purcell, so my 'Whispering Trumpet' was beginning to become known on records. Remembering back, I really think my desire to play a cornet began when I was very small, when my parents used to take Vera and me to a beach resort called Long Beach. Each afternoon and evening a big brass band would give concerts while the people sat on the sand listening. I remember my sister and I would build sand-castles while the band was playing, so you see I must have been pretty young. Anyway, I think that was what planted the seed, because I always watched the cornet players most of all, especially the man who played the melody. I was much more interested in him than the man who played the big bass. I loved to hear the music, not realizing at the time that I was listening to a band-master whose name would live for ever. He was a rather small man with a short white beard and I liked to watch him wave that stick he held in his hand. I wanted to do it too but I guess I was still just a bit young. They always played a piece of music I especially liked which the band-master had composed and each and every time I hear *Stars and Stripes Forever* I think of John Philip Souza.

One night at the Montmartre, while the Paul White-man Rhythm Boys were entertaining there and playing movie parties with my band, a man came in, I think especially to hear Bing Crosby. Bing finally did all his recording for this man called Jack Kapp, the Recording Manager for Brunswick Records. During the evening Jack Kapp called me over to his table and, on the spot, he signed me to start making Vocalian Records with my band. This was a subsidiary label of Brunswick Records. It started a friendship between Jack Kapp and myself which would last over the years, even until the time when later in London he was to form the

American Company, Decca Records, and he stayed at my house while he arranged the deal. It was Jack who signed a singing trio of girls I met on one of my trips to the Warner Brothers Radio Station one day while they were broadcasting. I looked in through a small window while these girls were singing, and what a terrific thrill I got. They were new and I had never heard of them before – they were on a level with the Rhythm Boys. What terrific arrangements! I noticed, when they were coming out of the studio, that one of them was in a wheel chair and the Studio Manager introduced me to them – The Boswell Sisters.

No wonder Jack Kapp had signed them for a recording contract. And it wasn't very strange that Bing Crosby and Connie Boswell made some records together – I know Bing thought she was great!

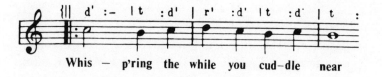

Whis — p'ring the while you cud–dle near

13. I Work For Fox Studios

XAVIER CUGAT was still my 'relief' band at the Montmartre and I remember that when I was playing for dancing he would sometimes go around to the different tables and sketch the stars, as he was an excellent cartoonist. He was in great demand, as his drawings were very good indeed. His music, although he had only around nine musicians, was first class and I used to like to sit and listen to him. He played the violin wonderfully and had a marvellous personality. It is easy for me to understand just why Cugat later became the outstanding attraction in Latin American music.

This was still only the beginning of sound films and the William Fox Studios were going to be equipped to meet the new demand. Through the recommendation of some song writers brought out from New York who had been signed by Fox, a man by the name of Ben Jackson called me out to the new studios in Westwood, just next to Beverly Hills, and said he had been put in charge of forming the Musical Production Department and, as he didn't know a note of music, he wanted me to give up my band to join him in its formation. This is hard to understand now, putting an unmusical man in charge of an operation like this, but he had been Studio Manager for several years and was an extremely good organizer. He told me I would have to become an executive and I would not be associated with the actual playing of music personally but would only act in the capacity of supervising everything pertaining to music. And they were planning many large-scale musicals. What a surprise this was.

Once again I had to make up my mind whether I was going to keep to band leading or try this new venture. The outcome was, I decided to accept this offer and soon I was in my own bungalow on the Fox lot wondering what it was all about. We planned a new building to be known as the Hall of Music and it wasn't long before it was built. It housed the Arranging Department, the Choral Department, the Musical Conductors and everything that was required for the making of Musical Productions.

One of my first assignments was the preparation of the *Fox Movietone Follies*. Stars, stars and more stars were brought out to California from the East for shows of this kind, and every film like this had several songs, dance production numbers, the star spots and the vocal choir. They all had to be orchestrated for, plus the arrangements for the studio orchestra to be conducted by Arthur Kay, our Musical Director. Of course, the first thing that took place was for the song-writers we brought out from the East to get cracking to supply all these tunes. Mostly they had been operating in New York or Chicago, but with the advent of the talkies, the studio became a goldmine for some of the top song-writing teams. We started to use so many songs in pictures that the studio formed its own song publishing company called the Red Star Music Company. There were so many songs that naturally they couldn't all be hits, so the final result was that eventually the Publishing Company folded. Well, by this time, I discovered I had taken a bit of a job on for myself. But it was probably the most interesting thing I have ever done. It was all so new at the time – pictures that really talked! Singers who really sang!

Yes, it was all very exciting. New stars were being born, for the first time singing stars with stage names, for many of the film personalities who had been successful in silent pictures weren't good for talkies, their voices weren't right. So the entire scene changed. Many name bands began to be used and, before long, we brought the Abe Lyman Orchestra out to Hollywood from the East for a film and Abe was more than happy when I went on to the set to see him. After all, he gave me my first big break and he always considered me as one of his boys. It was a strange turn of events – me being in the position of being *his* boss on this occasion.

I remember that after Abe had finished on the picture and had gone back to New York, we decided to re-shoot one of his scenes, so I took the same combination on to the same set and, in a 'long shot', was photographed with my back to the camera. I don't think anyone really knew the difference.

In my home in Beverly Hills I was listening to the radio one evening when I heard the most marvellous dance band. I didn't recognize it as any of the bands I knew, so I paid particular attention to this beautiful music. The arrangement was excellent and the whole thing made a great impression on me, so when the announcer said that it was a new record played by a British band I was truly surprised. It compared with most of the American orchestras, and the melody they played was one I hadn't heard before. But I have never forgotten hearing that record for the first time; it was made by Jack Hylton and was called *I Kiss Your Hand, Madame.*

For many years I had derived much enjoyment from listening to the great John McCormack on gramophone records, and when I heard the studio had arranged to bring him over to America from Ireland to make a picture, I was thrilled to think I would have the opportunity of meeting him. At last the day came and he was brought to my office so we could discuss plans for the film. He was quite a large fellow and was extremely congenial. The name of the production was going to be *The Rose of Tralee,* and that was easy to understand as it was one of his most famous songs. It transpired that the studio had built a small Irish type cottage right next to my bungalow for him to use while he was making the film, and now that I have visited Ireland so many times, I realize it was the real thing. Just exactly like those you can see in the southern part of Ireland, even to the 'peat' for the fireplace. The cottage had a low picket fence around it, with a lawn surrounding it and, of course, a thatched roof. John said it was just like being back home. In the small drawing-room was a piano so he and his accompanist could rehearse the music that was written especially. He also spent a great deal of time going over his lines, as speaking dialogue was something he hadn't done a great deal of.

It wasn't long before we were ready to start shooting and I don't think I have ever worked with a nicer person. It was a very hefty assignment, as there was a great deal of music connected with the production, all of which had to be orchestrated. The studio orchestra was enlarged for our Musical Director, plus the choral accompaniment which had taken a fair amount of time, but in the end the result was very worthwhile, as the film actually gave many millions of people a chance to see and hear John McCormack.

Speaking of John McCormack's cottage – each time the studio brought somebody out to Hollywood to star in a picture, the set designers made their glorified dressing-rooms authentically. In other words, in the case of John McCormack, his house was Irish, but when the famous cowboy, Will Rogers, arrived at the studio, he was accommodated in the most marvellous ranch-house, surrounded by sand and cactus. Just like something you would see in a film, one of the differences being, he had a built-in shower bath! He was another great guy and I spent a lot of my time on the set with him between shots. He, like some of the cowboys seen in pictures, liked to whittle a piece of wood while he was talking. His act consisted of just getting up and talking, mostly about politics, and he could keep people roaring with laughter for hours. He had made a big reputation doing this sort of thing in the Ziegfeld Follies on Broadway. His ranch-house was set up next to John McCormack's. Then when Beatrice Lillie was brought over from England to appear in a big musical we were making, naturally her dressing-room was strictly English. And that was the first time I ever met Bea, who was a great hit in the picture.

Around this time Hollywood, on account of all the work there was for musicians in films, was beginning to look like New York or Chicago where most of the big-time names in the dance band business had always operated. One night I was asked to go to hear a jazz fiddle-player who had just arrived in Hollywood and was playing in what we called a 'honky-tonk' – that is a club which didn't have a top rating. His name was 'Stuff' Smith – a very well known coloured guy who had mostly every night in the place a lot of the California musicians listening to him play. As you can guess, in the days before microphones, the fiddle player in a dance band would have a difficult time making himself heard while the trumpets and trombones, and not forgetting the saxophones, were blasting away. But 'Stuff' put this right by having a very small horn attached to his violin which picked up the sound and put him on a par with the rest of the gang. I think that was about the first time I had ever heard an instrument amplified. I for one was glad that he used that horn on his fiddle, for I would not have liked to have missed one single note of his fabulous playing.

One day I remember, when things were more or less quiet at the studio, I decided to go to Palm Springs where we had Xavier Cugat and his orchestra working on a picture which starred Victor McLaglen and a Mexican actress, Mona Maris. I thought it might be a good idea if I were to check up on what was going on and, at the same time, have a few days in the desert where Palm Springs is situated. Well, I took a studio car and driver and arrived late in the evening at a beautiful hotel built in Spanish style and owned by a former well-known young actress by the name of Fritzy Ridgeway. She was a terrific looking girl and I was delighted when she greeted me. In the patio there was the very inviting swimming pool and, as it was the height of summer, she asked me to have a swim. I joined her and it was one of the most refreshing swims I've had – even more so than when I used to go swimming at Santa Monica when I was a kid. Fritzy told me that if I wanted to go to the set before dinner she would show me how to get there, as it was right in the desert. When we arrived I remember, for some reason or other, the many millions of moths flying into the arc lamps being used to light the set. They were lying all over the ground underneath the lights. Victor McLaglen was surprised to see me and we planned to have a swim at the hotel as soon as he had finished shooting. Irving Cummings was a great friend of mine and he was directing. He held up taking the next scene while I went over to talk to Cugat who assured me everything was going well and I still remember how wonderful his music sounded out there in the still desert.

Cugat had made his orchestra a little larger by this time and by just listening to it I knew it was only a matter of time before he would really be going places. Which of course he did! But as soon as they completed the last 'take' Victor, Irving Cummings, Fritzy and I piled into the studio car and drove back to the hotel for a very welcome meal and the promised swim. After what was a most enjoyable evening, we all turned in and almost at the crack of dawn Fritzy knocked on my door and invited me for a ride – on horse-back! The only trouble with this was I'd never been on a horse before with the exception of 'Lonely' and the 'weenie' bake, and that didn't count. But she talked me into having a try, so after a quick breakfast we got on our way. She had fitted me out with some riding togs just a bit large (which didn't help any) and, as Palm Springs in those days was a tiny place, we were soon in the desert – that is, the start of it.

We had walked the horses up until that time, but the pace quickened soon and, although I was slightly scared, I did quite well considering. We rode out to a place like an oasis, where there were a few palm trees and a spring. It was really beautiful and the sun hadn't become too hot yet. We spent some time exploring and then we both enjoyed the lunch Fritzy had packed. As I had to get back to the set that afternoon we got on our way again and Fritzy asked me if I would like to have a race! Of course this was all I needed, as my bottom was already getting uncomfortable, plus the fact that my entire career on a horse was spent during the time we rode *out* to the oasis. But she explained that if I tried to gallop it was much easier staying on and, anyway, in case I fell off the sand was pretty soft. Well, as I wanted to make a good impression on this beautiful girl, I agreed and, to my utter amazement, I stayed on top, with the great help of the thing sticking up in front of the cow-boy saddle. Little did I realize at the time that one day I would be contemplating riding my own race horse in Britain as an amateur rider.

Palm Springs hadn't yet become the haunt of many well-known stars. It had very few small hotels and homes used mostly at weekends. When I got back to the location it was very hot and I was welcomed with a nice iced lager – there was a large tub full of it on the set. This, of course, was what is known as an exterior location and the street scene, especially built for this picture, was certainly the real thing – from the camera angle. It was a Mexican village and looked it. Cugat's music was being used for background for a song Mona Maris sang, but we also had a small Mexican group playing in a patio scene. I've always liked Mexican music and I still recall them playing and singing. It was about this time that Eddie Brandstetter, the owner of the Montmartre Cafe was opening a new place to be called the Embassy Club on Hollywood Boulevard, just next to the Montmartre. It was to be the most exclusive night-spot in town, which in fact it turned out to be. Eddie got me on the 'phone one day at the studio and asked me to come and see him at the Montmartre, which I did, not knowing what he had in mind at the time. We met and he asked me how I would like to form another band and play there. I told him I was contracted at the studio and my contract stipulated that I must not work with a band because of my executive position at the studio. But he painted such an enticing picture of what the new Embassy would be like that I promised to try to arrange it with the studio. Somewhat to my surprise, they okayed the suggestion and once again I was back in the band business. The Embassy was to be open only at weekends. All the catering was to be done from the Montmartre kitchens, which were right next door. I got a very good band together and it was a grand opening. Anyone and everyone who was in the 'Who's Who' of film business was there. In fact, many were turned away on the opening night! I was very happy to have my band again while still working at Fox studios and, being on weekends, it wasn't too tiring. By this time Paul Whiteman was back at Universal City working on *King of Jazz* with his orchestra, since the trouble which caused the delay in the film had been overcome, and as a special attraction Eddie Brandstetter talked Whiteman into appearing at the Embassy with the band for a short concert one night. The Rhythm Boys, Bing Crosby, Harry Baris and Al Rinker, were back with Paul now and it is really a wonderful memory. The full Paul Whiteman Orchestra played in what was a rather small intimate room, but I had never heard such music. What great strides this band had made since I first heard them on their opening night at the Alexandria Hotel in Los Angeles several years back. There have been such great bands since, but for my money, Paul Whiteman was greatly responsible for making popular music what it was in the hey-day of the Big Band.

My house in Beverly Hills was very near the famous Carthay Circle Theatre where many of the previews were held for outstanding new pictures. What great

days they were in the cinema! And to think I was at
Fox Films, right in the thick of it all! I really loved
those days; just to think this phase of my life had all
started not a stone's throw from the house in Beverly
Hills at the Los Angeles Country Club, where I had
played in the small dance band at the club on Saturday
nights. If anyone at that time had told me I would be
working at a Movie studio where they were making
motion pictures that talked, I would have thought they
were out of their mind. That was as far back as the year
1917 when I was sixteen years of age. At that time silent
movies had developed out of all proportion since the
real early days when I was a little boy. Yes, I've
experienced many of the first silent movies and even
played in dozens of them with my bands. I was part of
the scene when talkies arrived, and also appeared in
many of them and later starred with the band in
several. But how could anything I was connected with
possibly begin to compare with or surpass that wonderful train journey I made with my mother and dad in
that place of make-believe – Hale's Tours – so many
'flickers' ago.

During these moments when I am taking you back to
some of the early days I'm sure a lot of us would like to
recall, that is if you were around at that time, or even
if you're a bit too young to have known about the
actual happenings which took place, all of which went
to make up and create what we nowadays call 'old
movies' – I sincerely hope you will get a clear picture of
the kind of world I grew up in. It wasn't all roses but,
believe me, they were really exciting days. Yes, the early
Twentieth Century had wonderful surprises. Things we
take for granted now were just in the creative stage
when I was a kid. Somehow I think it was pretty good
then after all.

I remember being taken to a theatre where there was a musical show. I suppose it was the very first time I had seen the inside of a theatre. I know I was very small and while we sat in our seats all the lights went out and the big curtains drew aside and there before my very eyes I saw the most beautiful people up on the stage with great lights shining on them. They were all dancing around and kicking their legs in the air and singing songs. And when they stopped all the people sitting in the seats clapped their hands together. I did too and the people up there on the stage smiled, they liked it very much and bowed to us. Then a man came out on the stage and said some very funny things and made everybody laugh out loud. He had a big red nose and was real fat! Then during the show lots of girls and fellows were dancing together and my father told me that dance was called the *Texas Tommy*.

But let's get back now to the Fox Film Studios to see what happened next. About this time we were so busy at the studio with full-scale production that I was asked to take the studio orchestra and conduct the music on a picture we were about to make. The stars were my good friends, Janet Gaynor and Charles Farrell, the two people I told you about who had played together in such films as *Seventh Heaven* and several others as a new team, discovered by that wonderful director, Frank Borzage. Janet and Charlie by this time had become two of the top attractions on the Fox lot. They were very pleased when they knew I was going to be with the picture. When we started work we all remembered that I used to sit on the side-lines with my trumpet and play mood music for those first productions of theirs. And now here I was conducting the music for their first singing assignments. Neither of them was a great singer but they were very well liked by the public.

On quite a number of occasions when I was walking round the lot from one sound stage to another, or out on to what was known as the exterior lot where the huge sets were, such as street scenes, Western towns, or maybe a sea-port in China, I used to notice a fellow who was always looking around at things which were going on. He never seemed to be doing anything but looking. So one day I asked a director who this person was. He told me it was an actor the studio had brought out from the East to work in pictures but, although he was under contract, they hadn't given him anything to do yet. He just collected his salary each week but had to be on the spot in case something came up for him. He was a rather short man and certainly not the leading man type, but there he was, day after day, just hanging around. It wasn't too long before he started to get a break and went on to bigger things. His name was Humphrey Bogart! After serving in the Navy in the First World War, Humphrey Bogart went on the Stock Exchange and eventually went into films – in *The Petrified Forest*, numerous gangster films, and *The Maltese Falcon, Casablanca, The Treasure of The Sierra Madre* and *The African Queen* in which Katharine Hepburn starred with him.

Another person we had on the lot was a very cute little blonde who was featured in a few films. She was a terrific looking kid and was a good singer and dancer. Sometimes I would have a chat with her during filming and she was most likeable. Her name was Dixie Lee and she married a guy by the name of Bing Crosby.

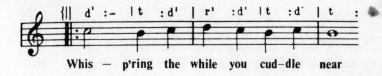

Whis — p'ring the while you cud–dle near

14. To London!

ONE DAY WHILE at the studio, I received a cable from London, England. It said: CAN YOU OPEN WITH BAND CAFE DE PARIS LONDON SEPTEMBER. EIGHT WEEK ENGAGEMENT. SEVEN PIECE BAND. WIRE CONFIRMATION. A lot of very strange things had happened to me so far, but I just couldn't begin to understand what this was all about. Naturally, I thought someone had made a mistake. How could they possibly know of me in England? It was all so mystifying, I didn't quite know what to do. But all at once I remembered that Abe Lyman and his Band were playing just down the street from my house at the Carthay Circle Theatre and Abe had been to London where he played at a place called the Kit Kat. Abe could put me right. I was soon in his dressing-room at the cinema and I was greeted at the door by Robert Montgomery, a well-known film star, who told me Abe was on stage. As soon as Abe came back I showed him the cable and he said: 'Hey, that is the top night spot in London.' I asked him what he thought I should do about it and he called into his dressing-room his personal manager Bob Goldstein (who later became Head of Twentieth-Century-Fox) and Bob scribbled out a message which I sent to London, and it clinched the deal. As it was only for a period of eight weeks, I thought the trip to London would be great and then I could return to the studio and treat it as an extended holiday.

But what about Dorothea? Then there was the thought of leaving Jean. Of course, if I could take Dorothea to London maybe all the excitement would help her forget the drinking, when she had other things to occupy her mind. If only it would do the trick, anything at all which might get her away from this horrible habit that was spoiling her life. Naturally, when I got up the courage to tell Jean about it, it was probably one of the unhappiest moments of my life and to have to hurt such a wonderful person was more than I like to remember.

When I told Dorothea about the offer she liked the idea very much and promised to try to stop what she knew in her sober moments was something which was ruining the wonderful happiness we had shared in the beginning. Now that that was settled, what about the band? I had always worked with a larger band than seven, so what was I to do? I didn't expect to make a big impression with such a small combination, but at least it should be fun. I remember that while I was at the Montmartre Cafe with my band, I had met a fellow from London called Jack Buchanan. He had been making a film – *Paris* – with Irene Bordoni at Warners and I got in touch with Jack and told him all about the offer. It was certainly the best place in London, he told me, Royalty and all that, and he thought I would do very well over there. Jack should know, he was a musical comedy star in London. As a matter of fact, Jack said he was building a cinema in the heart of

London which was going to be called the Leicester Square Theatre, and he had thought of asking me to bring an American band over to open it. But it would be some time before the cinema could be ready. Anyway, he told me he would certainly be at my opening night at the Cafe de Paris and sure enough he was. But we'll come to that later. While speaking of Jack Buchanan, I always considered him to be one of the nicest people I had met in show business. Jack played a most important part in my London appearance. But first things first! It didn't take me long to gather the band together and, as we didn't have a lot of time, I decided to rehearse on the boat on our way over.

We went to New York where we were booked on the Majestic, the largest ship at that time, which suited me right down to the ground as I thought the bigger the ship the less it would roll. We stayed in New York a couple of days before sailing and the one night we had we went to the Pennsylvania Hotel and heard the great band of Tommy Dorsey. What a great trombone player!

After hearing that kind of music I wasn't looking forward to what our band would sound like at the Cafe de Paris, but plenty of rehearsal, I felt, would help greatly. Yes, rehearsals – the only trouble was that the sea was so rough and the Majestic rolled so much that most of us were too sick to even think about music. And that is how we opened at the Cafe. What an ordeal! It's a good thing the boys in the band were the very best musicians I could muster together – they were all good readers and my singer was very good. And to make things worse we followed the great band of Hal Kemp that had made a very big hit.

Well, Jack Buchanan kept his word and was right there as he had promised in Hollywood. And what an opening night! I had never seen so many bejewelled ladies in a club and all the men were dressed in white tie and tails – that is, all except me. I and the boys in the band wore our very latest American tuxedos. I remember I had purchased a natty bow tie in New York for the occasion. It was very narrow (the latest thing in dress-wear) and it had a thin white line running across it. Really something! At the first break we had I went to Jack Buchanan's table. He was sitting with an American film director who was a friend of mine and Jack invited me to sit with them. Almost before we had had a chance to say Hello, Jack said how much he liked the music and, of course, I knew he was trying to make me feel good, but then he asked me if I minded him making a suggestion. I assured him I would be only too pleased because I realized the people dancing to our music weren't paying much attention. No-one actually said we were lousy but just nothing we played made any impression. Naturally I thought Jack was going to tell me how to rectify this sad state of affairs, but he leaned over and said: 'Roy, do you notice how all the gentlemen are dressed?' I said I did. 'I mean to say in white ties and evening dress and tail coats,' he said. I wasn't too sure what he was getting at but he put me right about this. He said that American tuxedos (or dinner jackets as he called them) were not worn in places of this kind and that the very next day I must meet him so he could take me to his tailor for a set of tails. He also asked me if I knew who the little fellow was who had come up to me to ask for a request number. I said I didn't know and Jack told me it was the Prince of Wales. I was naturally surprised, as I had never spoken to a real Prince before, but I had seen him in many Newsreel films showing him falling off his horse. Yes, the number Prince Edward had asked me to play was called *Without a Song*, so each and every time he came to the Cafe after that (which was nearly every night) he didn't have to ask for it, we automatically played it when we saw him coming down the staircase in this beautiful room where the cream of society danced nightly.

Sure enough I met Jack Buchanan the next day. He took me to his tailor and within a week (thanks to Jack) I was wearing my nice new white tie and tail suit and, almost immediately, during each evening at the Cafe, men would ask me where I had my clothes made. They would even send cards to the band stand enquiring who my tailor was. Lords, Dukes, the lot! It wasn't long before my name was being mentioned in the Press, most of the time referring to my tails, but not so much about my music. So you can understand just how important Jack's suggestion was to me, for in later years my dress clothes were almost as well known as my band. One night a dance band leader came in to see me and asked me to join him at his table. He said his name was Jack Hylton and he wanted to welcome me to England. His name rather startled me, as here was the same Jack Hylton I had heard on the radio in my home in Beverly Hills. Well, I was really pleased to meet him and it wasn't until he drove me to the theatre where he was playing for me to watch his show, that I realized his great popularity over here in Britain – and even on the Continent. Yes, Jack Hylton had the best stage-band entertainment I had heard, and he was a terrific show-man. I stayed in the wings while he was on stage and I remember the band bringing the house down.

I learned to have great respect for Jack and it wasn't until later that we were to become competitors. After I had been at the Cafe de Paris for a short time, a man came in to see me one evening and introduced himself. He had been in to hear the band several times and asked me how I would like to make some records for Decca? He said that a man named E R Lewis had just purchased the company and was going all out to make a very big success of it. This, of course, came as a great surprise to me because I figured the band hadn't set the world on fire at the Cafe de Paris and I had been a little disappointed at our reception, but still it figured. How could I expect to take London by storm with a 'pick-up' band, without the proper amount of rehearsals? So you can understand my surprise at receiving a proposition of this kind. And that was how I started to record for Decca, late in 1930 with my seven piece American band. The vocalist was Kenny Alan.

All my first records with the Company were made in the Chenil Galleries in King's Road, Chelsea. Decca was using this place for recording studios for quite a while, and the acoustics weren't all they should be – ever. One day we would go into the studio and part of the floor would be torn up or maybe a wall was being re-built or there were other hindrances – just trying to get the best recording effect possible. In those days we were lucky to have a microphone that worked properly. They never thought of using more than one microphone on a session. One mike to pick up the band and also the singers. Today, of course, practically every instrument is amplified. But we struggled through one way or another and our records began to sell. I made several records with my American band and now it was just about time for my contract with the Cafe de Paris to end, and I was beginning to think about getting back to the Studios in Hollywood to continue supervising music on the big musicals they were turning out. But one day I was called to see Mr Avidon, the man who first signed me up for the Decca contract. He said that Mr Lewis, the Managing Director, wanted me to stay in London and form an all British band and in addition be the Musical Director for Decca Records. This meant that I would have to send my American musicians back home, which was no hardship for them, as most of them had only come to London for the eight week 'holiday' and to see the place, but it also meant I would have to forego my job at Fox Studios. This really put me in a quandary. What was I to do? Mr Lewis said he would like me to stay and play our American type of music with the best musicians I could find and he would give me one hundred per cent publicity.

At that time the Musicians' Union were being very strict about foreign bands but, inasmuch as I would be leading an all British orchestra, he thought he could arrange it with the Home Office. Well, what was I to do? What a decision to have to make. Of course, I could always go back to the States later, although I didn't like the idea of giving up my job at Fox Studios. But again, that wasn't with my own band, just the Studio Orchestra on occasion when I would conduct music on a film. Of course, I hadn't been in this part of the world before and there was so much to see on the European continent. Mr Lewis said I could even broadcast from Paris after he started the Decca Hour on Sundays. That sounded pretty exciting, so why not! I guess I was superstitious enough to believe that I had received that cable in Hollywood for some good reason, so why not follow it through and have a go? I accepted the offer for which I was to be paid a certain amount each week as a retainer against the royalties from my records. Here was an assured income, which extended over a period of time and, as I was to provide Decca's number one band, naturally I would be receiving a great deal of publicity, which, of course, I did, both in Britain and on the Continent. Yes, it must be the right thing to do. So the next step was to go to Paris as soon as my contract at the Cafe de Paris ended and Decca arranged my labour permit to work in the British Isles and permission from the Home Office for me to stay. While this was being done a person had to leave the country if only for a few days before they could re-enter with the proper qualifications. That weekend in Paris was probably the happiest I have ever spent there. It was a beautiful sunshiny Spring and, after the London weather of practically nothing but fog, this was heaven. Especially as it was my first visit to Paris, this wonderful place I had heard so much about. The one thing I wanted to do I did, and that was to go and hear Maurice Chevalier in the music hall.

Back in London I started immediately to form my new recording band. First of all I had to find someone who knew the best musicians and could help me by suggesting the kind of boys I needed. I'd heard of a very fine arranger who was a pianist named Lew Stone, and a top drummer called Bill Harty. I got together with them and, after they had agreed to join me, they told me of a vocalist who had been out of work for quite some considerable time and was finding it pretty difficult to make both ends meet. I thought that if this singer was all that good why wasn't he working. But Lew and Bill pressed the point and, at last, I asked this man to come along and give me an audition. When he arrived, I noticed he made a good appearance – most necessary, of course – and he had a pleasing personality. Lew Stone accompanied him at the piano and when he started to sing I was sure he was the person I was looking for. His name was Al Bowlly. I soon made up the band with the best musicians I could find and we started turning out records for Decca by the dozen.

We recorded at least twice a week, making four titles

at each session and that was the very beginning of the hundreds and hundreds of discs I made during my career. The new band was an instant hit on records and, sure enough, I have never seen such publicity as Decca gave me. My photographs and records were in the windows of nearly every record shop, we had the full front page of the *Daily Mail,* and our records were played by the BBC almost every time you listened and also on the Continent. Yes, we were on our way. One of the very first things we did was a recording of *The Peanut Vendor.* It was just one of the many sides Al Bowlly did with that first band, which started him on the road to being one of the most famous of all British vocalists.

The Peanut Vendor was recorded in February 1931. So popular were our records becoming that one day I was asked by a man who was building a new club in the West End to come to see him. His name was Mr Upson and he owned the Dolcis Shoe Company. He told me the new club was going to be the smartest thing in London and would be exclusive. He said he had found when he went to other clubs they were generally too crowded to dance and that was why he was opening his own club so that he could provide a bit more comfort. He was going to call this new night spot The Monseigneur. It was right in the heart of Piccadilly. Would I be interested in opening with my band? He made it sound so worthwhile with the amount of money he offered and the fact that I wanted some place to be seen by the public apart from just making records, I had no hesitation in accepting. There would be only a few short weeks before the opening and there were one or two changes I intended making in the band. I engaged the brass section from the Billy Cotton Band and when it was time for the opening, the personnel in the band were Al Bowlly (vocalist), Lew Stone (piano), Bill Harty (drums), Don Stuteley (bass), Syd Buckman, Nat Gonella (trumpets), Joe Ferri (trombone), Ernest Ritte, Jim Easton, Harry Berly (saxophones).

Opening night was really something! The Prince of Wales, the Duke of Kent, King Alfonso (of Spain), they were all there and the room was decorated so beautifully. All the walls were dark blue and draped with red silk and a large painting of Monseigneur hung near the cocktail bar – very French and in the most excellent taste.

When thinking of Al, I can't help recalling that when we finished our first week and he received his first cheque, he was so happy to have had the chance of working again after so many ups and downs that to show his gratitude, he invited Dorothea and me for a meal in a little Italian restaurant in Soho. We went along with him and he ordered a very special dish he thought we would both like and during the course of this delicious chicken *entree,* I thought I heard a most peculiar kind of sound. After much detective work I discovered Al was chewing on a chicken bone. I queried this and he said: 'Boss' (he always called me Boss), 'haven't you ever tried chewing chicken bones? They're the best part and very good for the teeth.' Well, I knew Al had beautiful white teeth but I never realized how he kept them looking that way.

Just as Xavier Cugat was my relief band at the Montmartre Cafe in Hollywood, the relief band at the Monseigneur was a young violinist who was destined to go places with his Topica Tango Orchestra. Yes, it was Mantovani and even at that time I used to enjoy listening to his music. His fiddle playing was excellent and he was well liked by the dancers.

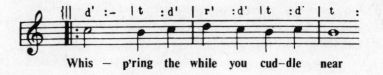

Whis — p'ring the while you cud-dle near

15. Clubs and Kings

EARLIER I MENTIONED I was playing at the Palace Theatre on Broadway in New York with Marion Harris, so being in London I thought I would go to see some variety shows over here. A friend of mine said that if I wanted to see the real thing he would take me to the Holborn Empire. I was looking forward to seeing a beautiful theatre and a great show. Upon arriving at the theatre, I was wondering just what kind of a place it was as it looked kind of delapidated to me, but in we went and when I got inside I couldn't believe my eyes. The theatre itself looked as though it had been built a very long time ago and there was just a small pit orchestra. The whole place wasn't very large, especially after seeing some of the variety theatres in the States. But soon the show went on and the reason I am telling this story now is because I don't ever remember when I was so struck as I was after seeing some of the acts which were so popular in the thirties. It was really Music Hall at its best! And never had I heard an audience showing its appreciation as they did during that performance. There was a very funny guy named Max Miller, then a couple of comedians called

Flanagan and Allen; two great acts who were to join me when I later started to play variety, and they never failed to 'stop the show' wherever they went.

My band was an overnight success at the Monseigneur, and almost immediately the BBC asked me to broadcast. After our very first broadcast I began to receive hundreds of letters from all over the country and from what at that time was known as the British Empire. Every Wednesday night from ten-thirty till twelve o'clock was Roy Fox night on the 'air'. That lasted for years. The band soon became one of the best sellers on records and then I was approached by Earl St John, head of the Paramount Cinema chain, to put my band on the stage of the Paramount Cinema in Regent Street, Piccadilly. In those days, they had what was known as Cine-Variety, meaning that my band played the first half of the show, followed by the film. It didn't take long to get our act together and we opened to a great success. Yes, things were going along very nicely indeed. That is, until I was taken ill with pleurisy. I remember that week, we were playing on the stage of the Carlton Cinema, in addition to our job each night at the Monseigneur, and it was necessary for me to have a doctor in my dressing-room all that week to keep me going. It was slightly difficult to blow a trumpet while having pleurisy, and all this, added to the fact that we had to rehearse for our weekly broadcasts and recording sessions, forced my doctor to say that if I didn't take time off for a good rest he would not be responsible. He suggested Switzerland. This was substantiated by the King's physician, so the only answer was for me to follow his advice. I left Lew Stone in charge of the band while I was away, which my boss found satisfactory, and I went to a very small village up in the Alps to rest and recover from my illness. Every Wednesday night I listened on my little radio on the top of the mountain to my band broadcasting in London. After each broadcast I would telephone Lew to discuss the programme with him. I must say, he kept everything going well while I was away. After five months I had the okay from my Swiss doctor and returned to London. I got a great welcome when I joined the band again and picked up where I had left off. I promised to take it easy, but again it wasn't long before I was working just as hard as before. One of the first things I accepted was an offer to play at the Palladium, and the engagement proved a further huge success. The reviews were great and the show went down like a million with the audience.

The broadcasts continued to bring lots and lots of fan mail and we were packing them in at the Monseigneur. Around this time, a very young girl came to me and asked me if she could have an audition as a singer. She was quite small and she said she was sixteen years old. I have never heard an accent quite like hers. It was a mixture of broad Scots and American. The audition was arranged and, when I heard her sing, there was no doubt in my mind that this kid was really terrific. She was on the bandstand with the boys and myself before she knew it. She recorded with us and, believe me, she was well ahead of her time. I couldn't understand where this small Scots lassie had learned to sing like that. I wasn't very far wrong in my estimation of her, as she later became one of the top singing stars in America. She starred in several films and the last time I saw her in New York was when I visited her dressing-room at the Loew's State Theatre on Broadway. She was 'head-lining the bill'. It must run in the family, for she was Jimmy Logan's aunt. Her name, of course, was Ella Logan.

About this time my contract at the club was about to be renewed, but when it came to discussing it with the owner, it transpired we couldn't agree on terms. I thought the band had earned more money through its popularity, but he didn't seem to think so. The outcome was, I decided to leave. I told the boys in the band that evening after work that we would be leaving and, of course, they were surprised. A couple of nights later, they all asked me to meet them after work and they told me that Lew Stone had been approached by the management to remain on at the Monseigneur and, inasmuch as they didn't know where I would be going with the band, they decided to remain. That is, all except my trumpet player and vocalist, Syd Buckman. I'm sure the boys thought if I lost the Monseigneur I was finished. Well, it didn't turn out that way at all. By the time I had completed my contract, I had found an entirely new band and opened the following night at the Cafe Anglais in Leicester Square. I kept up my broadcasts on Wednesday nights and once again the new band carried on as if nothing had happened. The fan mail increased and many of the people who had danced to my music at the Monseigneur started coming to the Anglais. This was a great relief. As everything had happened so suddenly, I hardly had time to think how it would all turn out. One night at the Anglais a man who was very tight danced by me and stopped to ask me if I would like to take the band to Belgium to play a Royal Command Performance for King Albert. Just to appease him I said: 'Sure, I'd like to.' I thought this might make him happy, so he seemed satisfied and danced on his merry way. I had no more trouble with him that evening. He was a very happy character, the kind I ran into on many occasions, and generally, if you used a little tact, everything would go smoothly. He was dressed nicely in tails, but his button-hole carnation looked like someone had stepped on it.

I didn't give it any more thought until one evening this same man came in to see me and this time he was stone cold sober. He came over to the bandstand and said: 'Well, Roy, I've fixed everything.' I said: 'What do you mean?' He said he had arranged for me to fly to Brussels to play the Royal Command Performance for King Albert which he had mentioned the other evening! He said: 'I assume you can get away from here for the night.' I told him I thought he was kidding, especially since he had been slightly under the weather. He assured me he knew everything he did and said when he'd had only a couple of drinks. Then I asked him why they had chosen my band and he said the King listened to the radio very often and that I was his favourite. He also had a good number of our recordings. Just to think, a real honest to goodness King playing my records. This was just too much, especially for an American, as we don't see Kings every day. This was real story book stuff. Probably more so because I had never really got used to the fact that I had been thrown into the great big world of glamour at such an early age, and from a very modest family. Meeting great stars long before I knew what life was all about. Hob-nobbing with millionaires and society. And now this! I was already nervous.

Now the outcome of that was that the band and I flew to Brussels in two planes and played for the Royal Family at the Agora Cinema in Brussels at the premier of a film showing. I shall never forget it; we played an hour show which met with great approval from the audience. I don't think I have ever seen more jewels glittering and everyone was, of course, dressed in evening wear. After our performance the house lights went up and the theatre manager came down through the centre aisle and asked me to accompany him. We went up to the Royal Box in the Dress Circle and the Royal Family stood up as I was presented to them. I don't suppose I have ever been so taken aback during my life time. The Queen asked me if my band was all British and I said everyone was except me; I was American. She said: 'Oh, Albert, we love America, don't we?' He said: 'Yes, my dear.' Then she introduced me to Prince Leopold and Princess Astrid and some Ladies-in-Waiting. Everything in the cinema was as quiet as could be while this was taking place and finally I said good-night and thanked them.

Then when I got back to the stairs of the dress circle, I stumbled on the first step and nearly fell on my face while everybody was applauding and saying 'Bravo!' I guess that was my most embarrassing moment. Then, right after the Royal Show, we played at a big dance given in honour of the Command Performance and it was a wonderful affair. So many people told me how much they had enjoyed our performance. I was very pleased to know my new band had been such a success. And when we arrived back in London we found that we had hit the headlines.

Soon after this, I was approached by the owners of Gaumont-British Pictures, who owned the famous Kit Kat Club, to see if I would consider going into the Kit Kat on a year's contract. It didn't take much thought on my part, for I felt that it would give me the chance to enlarge my band even further, and they promised me that if I signed up I would be featured with my band in some of their films. This clinched the deal and before long I opened at the Kit Kat. It was a large room with a balcony and many world famous American bands had played there, including the Abe Lyman Band. I enlarged my band to seventeen pieces, including myself, and the club built a bandstand to my order. There was a separate little platform for each musician, and the effect was most impressive. Again I kept my usual night for broadcasting and I got wonderful publicity in all the Gaumont-British cinemas. The personnel of the band now was Syd Buckman, Les Lambert, Andy Hodgkiss (trumpets), Eric Tann, Miff Ferrie (trombones), Art Christmas, Hughie Tripp, Harry Gold, Rex Owen (saxophones), Jack Nathan (piano-arranger), Ivor Mairants (guitar), George Gibbs (bass), Maurice Burman (drums), Jack Plant, Peggy Dell, Ronnie Genarder, Syd Buckman and The Clubs (vocalists).

All this happened in 1933 and before long a friend of mine told me he knew a young boy who could sing extremely well and he would like me to hear him. This boy was an electrician, but he wanted to join a dance band, so I arranged to hear him. He sounded pretty good, but I told him that if he would study voice training for a while, there would be a good chance of his coming with me. He did as I suggested and later when he came back, I signed him up. His name was Denis Pountain but we agreed to change it to Denny Dennis. Denny soon began to make a name for himself on my broadcasts and the records and I knew his success was assured.

The famous Val Parnell, who was Head of the Palladium, asked me to appear at the Royal Command Performance of 1933. This, I suppose, was the crowning glory of my entire career. Until that time I was the only American band leader to receive this honour and that, of course, was because my band was all British. Well, after recently playing for the Royal Family in Belgium, then having this happen, I was more than glad that I decided to stay in England and not go back to the Fox

Studios. I must confess I was really excited.

Well, the big night finally arrived and what a wonderful sight it was to walk out on to the stage of the Palladium again, only this time there up in the Royal Box sat King George and Queen Mary! Here I was playing before the King and Queen, and when I had to walk up to that microphone and say: 'Your Majesties, Your Royal Highnesses, Ladies and Gentlemen, good evening!' I was sure my tails weren't hanging straight or my white bow tie was crooked, but after our first number, the reception made up for everything. It was wonderful and I even saw the King applauding. After our band show Miss Evelyn Laye came on and sang while we played for her. She was so beautiful and was such a great favourite with the public.

It was certainly a glamorous night – Marlene Deitrich saw to that. When she walked on to the stage she stopped the show cold and it was a while before she could continue with her spot. After the performance I was introduced to her by a friend of mine, Douglas Fairbanks, Jr.

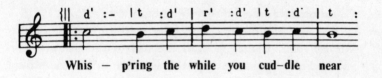

Whis — p'ring the while you cud-dle near

16. Touring

A PRODUCER FRIEND of mine came in to see me one evening at the Kit Kat and invited me over to his table. His name was Sam Smith and he told me he had recently finished a film called *Radio Pirates* and that he had been having great difficulty selling it for distribution, it was so 'lousy', he said, to use his exact words. How would I like to go out to the British Lion Studios with my band and do three or four numbers which would be put into the picture and see if that would help? We arranged a deal and much to everyone's amazement, and to show how popular the band had become, the film was not only sold on the strength of our band being in it, but it broke all records. That was just one of several movies we appeared in.

At the Kit Kat there was the usual 'relief' band. In this case it was a young band leader, Joe Loss. Joe played good music. I have great respect for him because from that day he has done nothing but climb the ladder of success. He has always kept just ahead and has continued to grow in popularity. That is a long time to remain at the top of the tree.

One night I was introduced to one of the top

greyhound trainers at Wembley Stadium. While talking to him at the table I asked him about the dogs he trained, and he started to tell me such interesting stories about the dogs he ran in the Greyhound Derby and such races that I began to wonder if this was not a truly remarkable way to put myself in a financial position whereby I could associate with all those lucky people who spent most of their time in the South of France. If I bought the right dog through the assistance of my new acquaintance, all that would be left for me to do would be the great pleasure of betting on it, then find myself watching the horrified expression on the face of each of the bookies as I nonchalantly stuffed my pockets with the cash he counted out in fivers.

It was rather an early age to think of retiring, but I could always have another band – maybe one to play just for my own amusement. I asked Arthur – his name was Arthur Callanan – if he could find me a dog. He said he knew the very one. It was on a farm in Ireland and he would arrange to have it brought over at once.

It was a wonderful thrill when I went out to the Stadium to meet the beautiful black dog which I named 'Whispering Symphony'. The dog liked me because Arthur let me give him some hamburger and each time I went to visit him and play with him on the grass in the centre of the Stadium, where they play the Cup Final, he expected the same tasty morsel.

Of course he was new to the track and Arthur had to teach him what it was all about. Then came the night he was to run for the first time. I couldn't wait to collect that first lot of hundred pound notes and, although Arthur slyly mentioned the fact that I should 'take it easy' the first time, I thought I might as well not waste any time. And did Whispering look terrific. He was hopping all around the place as they paraded around the track.

I was rather flattered to see that some of the bookmakers knew me and, of course, realized they were only being friendly by letting me have such big odds. I felt a bit ashamed of myself when I put down quite a good-sized bet (for me) and hoped it wouldn't cause the bookmaker too much hardship when my dog won.

By this time, the dogs were going into the traps and before I knew it, the doors burst open and out flew all the dogs at a great pace – all except mine! He didn't seem at all interested in the proceedings. I was standing next to the bookmaker so that I could collect my winnings quickly, and he said, 'Hard luck, Roy!'

This I couldn't believe! Something must have gone wrong. When I joined Arthur he said that sometimes this happened with a new dog the first time in the trap and, knowing him to be one of the finest trainers in London, I realized it was only a matter of time until I'd get that money back – plus! After all, maybe I had been a little greedy – even to the extent of purchasing some more dogs so that I could call it my 'string' (I thought that sounded good) – and the more winners the more money.

I thought that was the best idea I ever had, but before long I was wondering if I'd be seeing Monte Carlo until my next holiday. This game was harder than I had thought. My dogs won their fair share of races but not enough for my early retirement.

PS Whispering Symphony lost the Scottish Greyhound Derby Final by a 'whisker'.

While at the Kit Kat, I made friends with Duke Ellington. That was when he came over to London to play at the Palladium. Ellington brought Jazz from the back streets of New Orleans for the world to hear it and enjoy it. His real name was Edward Ellington, he was called Duke because he was always well dressed. He composed a great deal of delightful music, including *Mood Indigo* and *Sentimental Lady*; he also played sacred music, and was one of the most brilliant pianists.

He said he had heard about my band and he wanted to come in to hear us and to say Hello. I had not met him before in the States and, of course, I was a great admirer of his orchestra and especially of the numbers he had written. You couldn't ask to meet a nicer guy and when I introduced him to some of the boys in the band they were overjoyed. They had met the 'great' Ellington at last. Later on in New York I was to continue this friendship with him.

The same thing happened when Cab Calloway came to London. He too paid us a visit, and he invited me over to the Palladium to see his show – he was a really amazing character. What a showman! And, of course, his 'scat' singing was all the craze. About this time, Decca asked me to fly over to Paris with the band to do an hour's broadcast on their Decca Hour which took place every Sunday afternoon. We took Jessie Mathews over in the plane and she sang a number with us. She was a very big Cochran star then, and had starred in several films. I was more than pleased to have her appear in the show.

It is one flight in a plane that I vividly remember. On the return crossing, we had just about reached the Channel when, looking through the window, I noticed some oil streaming out of one of the motors. Of course, this was quite some time before jets, and the more I watched the oil, the larger grew the spot on the wing. It was snowing very hard and when we started to lose altitude I had visions of the oil catching fire with a resulting crash. I also was sure the loss of height was caused by the inefficiency of the propeller; how could it work properly when it was in such a weakened condition due to the loss of power? The oil slick started to cover quite a large area of the wing and I knew it was just a matter of moments until the end came. But we did manage to limp back to the airfield at Croydon and when we disembarked we were met by the Newsreel cameramen; and, as the pilot was also asked to join us, I asked him just how serious the oil leak had been, and how close we had come to disaster. He calmed my nerves when he explained that the oil I had seen was caused by a surplus in the motor.

Of all the British dance bands, Ambrose, Harry Roy, Billy Cotton and the others, I always considered Bert Ambrose my hottest competitor. He played the kind of music I liked and he had a very fine orchestra. We were good friends and I had great admiration for him. He catered strictly to the 'class' trade and I feel we always tried to out-do each other. He had an excellent vocalist called Sam Browne and I'm sure many of you will remember the band's broadcasts and their records.

Early in 1934 I moved to the Cafe de Paris again from the Kit Kat and it was one of the nicest rooms I had ever played in. It was very different now from the time when I first opened there with my American gang. So much had happened in such a comparatively short time. Here I was with a reputation, making good money, owning my first Rolls Royce, living in a beautiful house on Hampstead Heath – yes, it was all happening. Fan mail was increasing with every post and they were very happy days indeed. With the exception, unfortunately, of Dorothea; she was steadily growing worse in spite of her good intentions. By this time the management of the Cafe was bringing over from the States some of the top acts for cabaret, and who should

open there but my old friend Marion Harris. It was
strange that our paths had crossed so many times in the
past and here we were again. I must say, I was really
glad to see her, and her opening was absolutely sensational. She certainly took London by storm! Her
dressing-room every night was full of Royalty, society,
and many people who wanted to wine and dine her.

Then once again, who should turn up but Sophie
Tucker. As a cabaret artiste no one could beat her. The
faithful Teddy Shapiro was still with her at the piano
and her success matched that of Marion Harris.
Working with Marion and Sophie again made it seem
like 'old home week'. Even after being in London for
three years, it still seemed a little strange to me and it
was nice to meet them once more. Naturally Sophie tore
the place apart as she always did everywhere she appeared. A very great star and a warm-hearted person.

I don't think I mentioned how I happened to come to
the Cafe de Paris from Hollywood. It transpired that a
friend of mine, Dorothy Mackail, a star in pictures in
Hollywood, who had been at Fox Studios while I was
there, was in London on holiday. She was in the Cafe
de Paris one evening and the manager asked her if she
knew of an American band they could get to follow Hal
Kemp when he left to return to the States. Dorothy said
she knew the very best – Roy Fox. The manager said he
had never heard of Roy Fox. Dorothy told him that my
band was very popular in Hollywood and I was most
certainly the one he should get. Knowing what a good
salesman Dorothy was when she had a couple of drinks,
she helped on the spot with the wording of the cable to
me which was to change my life completely. Then Jack
Buchanan, who had met me in Hollywood when he was
working on a film, could have convinced the manager
that he had done the right thing sending for me. Now

here I was, at the Cafe de Paris for the second time, and going along very nicely when I was offered a tour of the Variety Halls with the band. The deal was one I could not afford to refuse, so very kindly the management of the Cafe de Paris agreed to let me accept. And on 21st May 1934 we opened at the Empire Theatre, Glasgow.

That was just the beginning of what developed into five years of highly successful and profitable touring of the Variety theatres of Britain and the Continent. Our opening at the Empire Theatre, Glasgow, was an outstanding hit with the public, who were just waiting to see and hear the band they had listened to on the radio. I must say, I had a wonderful bunch of boys in the band, who not only played good dance music, but were great performers on stage. Our reviews were all .one could wish for, and our success increased as time went on. I was told that Gracie Fields and my band were the top attractions in Variety. Never shall I forget the reception we received when the 'tabs' went up that first night. What a wonderful feeling to think we were so well liked before we even started our show. But as the opening applause was terrific, it's hard to describe the acclaim at the finish. We could hardly get off the stage. All this as the result of our Wednesday night broadcasts from the West End of London. Then, when I was leaving the theatre, I was overwhelmed by the crowd at the stage door waiting for autographs. My poor chauffeur was somewhat overcome by the fact that people were climbing all over the Rolls, to be able to see better. What a wonderful feeling! I then knew why I had been given the foresight to remain in Britain. I was superstitious enough to think that the cable I received at the Fox Studios in Hollywood had been sent me for some good reason that I couldn't really understand at the time. But this was it! Until now I had wondered if

I had done the right thing by giving up my job as Head of the Musical Production Department of Twentieth-Century-Fox to live in Britain; but there was no doubt in my mind now. It was my custom, when playing the Music Halls, to take a percentage of the gross admission fees and I would then be responsible for the payment of, not only my band, but all the artistes appearing on the bill and I remember that first week, after I had paid everyone, including my managers and travelling expenses, etc, I was more than happy with what was left over. It was so much more than I had been used to making in the West End of London in the clubs, I was most pleasantly surprised. Especially when it continued each week as we toured over a period of years.

Denny Dennis by this time was getting more and more popular with audiences and his voice had improved greatly. I think he was starting to forget that he had been an electrician and was now rapidly becoming aware of the possibility that he may one day be top vocalist of Britain, which, of course, he was. I'm sure it would have surprised him to know that one day he would be singing with the great Tommy Dorsey band in the States.

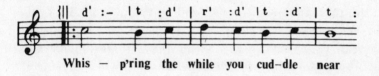

Whis — p'ring the while you cud-dle near

17. Back to the States

ONE OF THE old-timers who used to play the halls with us was Will Fife. Will was a wonderful character and we became good pals. He used to take me fishing on Loch Awe or Loch Ness when we were in Scotland and we had some marvellous times together. I used to love to fish, ever since my mother and I spent so much of our time sitting on the pier at Santa Monica. One night, after one of our performances at the Glasgow Empire, I was having a late supper at the hotel and 'Sandy' Trotter, the Editor of the *Express*, heard me remark that I was keen on fishing. He excused himself for a moment and brought back from another table a friend who said Sandy had mentioned that I liked fishing. He invited me to go to Loch Lomond the next morning as he had a boat on the Loch and he thought we may come across a salmon or two. This I liked; so, bright and very early, we pushed off from the bank out on to this beautiful stretch of water. I was naturally thrilled at the prospect, having never hooked a salmon. It wasn't long before we were quite a way from the shore and on about the second cast, my friend, who was a doctor, had a terrific 'strike' and what an exciting moment it was. He played the fish for a short while, and once in a while we could just see this silver object in the water and, of course, it had to happen, it got away. What a disappointment! But we both expected another to be along at any moment and once again his reel started to sing and this time it seemed to be an even larger salmon; so large, in fact, it was much too strong and my friend met with the same fate. We continued to fish for a little while and the doctor said he thought it may be wise for us to move to a place nearer the opposite bank as 'that great big black cloud up there' looked a bit threatening. It was just as well we did, because just as he mentioned that several people had lost their lives on the Loch, a sudden storm blew up. No sooner had we reached a spot just a few yards from the bank than the waves started washing over us and the boat partly capsized. We just made it to the shore, and was I glad? Aside from being frightened I was also sick, which I can assure you is a bad combination on such an occasion. A car picked us up and I just made it back to the Empire in time to change and walk onto the stage feeling rather lucky to hear the strains of *Whispering* once more.

About this time I ran a national vocal contest to try to find a girl singer for the band – the winner to receive a contract. Every place we played I would audition anyone who wished to enter the contest. Over a period of several months I must have heard hundreds of aspirants, but the outcome of this search was quite startling. It all happened when I was in Glasgow on one of our return engagements at the Empire there. I had tied up with the Scottish *Express,* who helped organize the contest there, and in a small hall in their building I noticed that one of the contestants was a tiny girl thirteen and a half years old. I couldn't believe my ears when I heard her sing the songs she'd prepared for the

audition. Here was this little Scots kid singing in broad
American with more style than I had heard yet; and
what a terrific style she had – I couldn't understand
where she had picked it up. I immediately knew this
was the girl I had been looking for. But only thirteen
and a half! I selected her to enter the contest final
which was to be held that week on the stage of the
Glasgow Empire. The other regional winners were
brought from all over the country and, as far as I was
concerned, it was a foregone conclusion. Sure enough,
May McDevitt won it hands down. May McDevitt –
something would have to be done about that name, so
I decided to call her Little Mary Lee. I arranged to
have her aunt travel with her as chaperone and she was
an immediate sensation. So much so that later she was
to be voted the number one girl vocalist of Britain by
the magazine *Melody Maker*. I must point out that in
those days it was very difficult to find a really good
singer. I had been lucky to find an electrician, Denny
Dennis, who reached the top spot, and then this little
girl.

During that year, 1935, I went to the States for a
holiday so that I could see my mother whom I hadn't
seen for several years. While aboard ship I received a
cable from Paul Whiteman and Rudy Valee welcoming
me back to America. Rudy Valee's car was waiting to
take me to my hotel; and my meeting with my mother
was something I shall never forget. It was her very first
time in New York and when she looked out of the
window of her room at the Waldorf Astoria Hotel she
couldn't realize those moving objects down there on the
road were people – we were on the sixty-fifth floor. And
one of the first things I did was to go out to Rudy
Valee's home on Long Island one evening for dinner
after which he and I sat on the floor while he showed

me his colour films – mostly of his hunting lodge in Maine. Alice Faye was the vocalist with his band at the Woodmanston Inn where he was playing, and later he drove me to that beautiful club, which was packed to capacity when we arrived. Rudy, who was one of the very top personalities of the band business at that time, always sang through a megaphone, and he was one of the biggest sellers on records.

Alice Faye was not only sensational with the band, she was also really very beautiful. A lovely person! When she sang everybody gathered around the bandstand to listen, and I wouldn't be surprised to hear that's just what Phil Harris was doing before they were married. I must say Rudy Valee made my ten days' stay in New York most pleasant. He loaned me his car to get around in and he was a really wonderful guy. While there Paul Whiteman invited me to have lunch with him at the exclusive Colony Club. He naturally wanted to know what had happened to me while in London. He had heard, he said, of my success. After hearing hundreds of his recordings for years, he said at lunch: 'Roy, do you remember what the very first record was I made?' Of course, I couldn't remember, and when he said it was *Whispering* I nearly fell off the chair. He said he thought it might surprise me, as he knew I had been using *Whispering* as my signature tune for years.

Irving Aaronson was in New York at that time. He was playing at a beach resort with his 'Commanders' and he invited me to bring my mother for a day's outing. It was a place where the bathers could sit in deck-chairs on the sand and listen to his concert. His band played in a small bandstand. There were thousands of people gathered round and Irving introduced me as a band-leader from England and asked me to conduct his band in a number. I noticed my mother was very proud of me and maybe it took her back to the time when she probably had great difficulty in finding the eleven dollars so that I could have that little cornet I had set my heart on.

Before leaving New York to return to London I went to hear Guy Lombardo at the Commodore Hotel where his band was billed as 'The Sweetest Music this Side of Heaven'. I never completely agreed with this but he probably made more money than most band-leaders.

The other bands I went to hear on my last night in New York were Kay Kayser and the band billed as 'Swing and Sway with Sammy Daye'. Both were very popular at the time. Kay Kayser was a terrific show-man, he appeared with his band in a big TV show over the national 'hook-up'.

Sammy Kaye was extremely popular in the hotel where he was playing and also for his Saturday after-noon broadcasts. Those broadcasts gave you the impression that you were dancing in the very room in which the band was playing – it created a terrific atmosphere. Tea-dances were organized all over the country – needless to say it was a great gimmick.

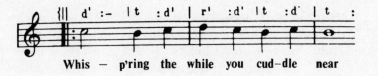

Whis — p'ring the while you cud–dle near

18. Pinfire

WELL, I MUST say, although it was wonderful seeing my
mother again and I had a most exciting time on my
brief holiday in New York, it was really good to be back
in London. By this time I had grown very fond of
London and to this day I don't think I would be happy
anywhere else. So it wasn't long before the band and I
picked up where we had left off and returned to playing
variety, Sunday concerts, broadcasting every Wednesday night, making gramophone records and playing
late-night dances. The band was such a happy bunch of
boys that it was a real pleasure working with them. The
work didn't seem nearly so hard and I remember those
days as days of real enjoyment. Of course, if the public
hadn't liked us so much I'm sure it wouldn't have been
nearly so much fun.

I had a very good friend named James Shand who
owned the White City Greyhound Stadium at Liver-
pool and, aside from owning many greyhounds, he ran
quite a number of race horses. One week when the band
was playing at the Empire Theatre, Leeds, Jim asked
me if I would like to drive to Middleham to see some
new horses he had just acquired. As I was living in

Harrogate for that week, it wasn't such a long journey to Middleham where Sam Armstrong and his brother, Gerald, trained their horses. It was a very famous training establishment. I arrived there one cold winter morning and found Jim already there. After a nice hot breakfast Jim, Gerald (his trainer) and I went out to the boxes housing the horses and made a tour of inspection – at least they both made the inspection and I just looked on, not knowing one end of a horse from the other.

When we came to one of the horses Jim told me he had just purchased it, and I liked the appearance of it very much. Jim said its name was Pinfire. I ventured near enough to pat it and inasmuch as it didn't kick me, I thought it was a mighty fine horse indeed. I guess Jim must have noticed how well Pinfire and I got on together because he said: 'How about going into the house and choosing your racing colours?' Naturally I enquired what he was talking about and he said he had just made me a gift of the horse! I was really flabbergasted and the outcome was that I then and there on the spot selected my colours. Needless to say, Jim could well afford to do such a nice thing as he had plenty of others in his string, but it isn't every day a friend gives you a race-horse. I was beside myself with excitement. Jim, by the way, had a horse called Thankerton who ran third in the Derby the year Mahmoud won. Thankerton had thrown up his head at the post and momentarily knocked out his jockey and he didn't really come to until just after Tattenham Corner, where he was leading the field by a good twenty lengths. Thankerton was just pipped near the winning post.

But, whereas Thankerton had been beaten, I was quite sure Pinfire would do the trick the following year when he was a three-year-old. But Jim told me he didn't think Pinfire had a great deal of chance of doing what a horse which had cost many thousands of pounds failed to do. I was inclined to disagree.

We entered him in the first race at Lincoln the following spring and I prepared to wait through the hard winter months before I could see Pinfire show his fellow entrants a thing or two. I immediately engaged the King's jockey, Freddie Fox (a good friend of mine), to ride and finally the dreary months passed.

I had forgotten to arrange a date for the band near the race course during that week and consequently the band had been booked at the Palladium in London. That meant, to see Pinfire run his first race, I had to go by car to an airport in the direction of Lincoln and hire a small plane to fly me to the course. It was the only way I could possibly have made it there and back in time. Well, the pilot and I took off in the beautiful sunshine, which I thought was a very good omen. After flying for about five minutes we encountered a fog which not only caused the pilot some concern but made it impossible for him to know where we were. I could have done without this bit of information. Then the pilot got the bright idea of dropping down a bit so that he might try and pick up the railway tracks which he knew were somewhere around. Fortunately he was successful in locating them. He said there should be an army airfield nearby, and was I glad when we touched down. The mechanic who was refuelling while we were waiting for the fog to subside, very kindly told the pilot it was just as well we had come down when we did, as the carburettor wasn't everything it should be. Not too daunted by this, I tried to get a car to take me to the course, but the unhappy end was, it couldn't be done in time. Upon arrival at the stage door of the Palladium I learned over the 'phone from Freddie Fox that Pinfire had been bumped out at the first bend and he had to settle for sixth place. Luckily, though, my beautiful horse did win several races for me. And each time I arrived at a theatre where we were going to play, the backstage hands would always say: 'Hello, Roy, how's Pinfire?

During this period we were asked to make a tour of Holland playing at dances and concerts. I remember especially rehearsing the kind of music I thought the Dutch people would like to hear at the concerts. We played a place called Haarlem and I was very surprised that, during the first two or three numbers I had especially prepared for them, the response wasn't all that terrific. In fact, they practically sat on their hands. I knew there was something wrong somewhere so I thought I would try *Tiger Rag* and no sooner had we finished than the crowd began to whistle and throw their programmes in the air with delight. Of course, I had no idea that that was the kind of music they would like. They were strictly 'with it' and during the remainder of the concert I cannot remember any audience ever being more appreciative. I didn't think the Dutch people could be so excited by anything.

There was just a little incident which happened to me during that tour in Holland that caused me a slight bit of embarrassment. I believe I have mentioned before that my tail suit was a great talking point in the press when they mentioned my name. Well on this occasion, my chauffeur, who always took care of my clothes while travelling, did his usual good job of packing my bags – that is, he packed everything on this occasion except my dress shirts, shoes, white ties, etc. I didn't realize until I started to dress for the performance and, inasmuch as it was Sunday in this rather small town, there was nothing to do but to try to find the man who owned the small men's shop nearby.

Someone finally discovered his whereabouts and I was outfitted with the most peculiar looking square toed shoes which were three sizes too large; then the collar they brought me was only about one inch high with great big wings, and the tie was very narrow and much too long. Well, when I walked out on to the stage and the band saw me they had to stop playing our signature tune *Whispering* for my entrance. Of course, the audience didn't know just what was happening, so there was nothing for me to do but to explain to the people. I'm sure I couldn't have looked funnier if I had tried, but those were the kind of things that kept the band in top gear all the time. Our child singer Mary Lee was a very big hit-wherever we went and this time was no exception.

While still in Holland we did a broadcast from Hilversum and it was quite amazing the amount of fan mail I received when we returned to London. The Dutch people really liked our music and this was made very clear when we were invited to play at the Concert Hall in Amsterdam – this was the hall in which Furtwangler played all his concerts with the symphony orchestra. The next day after our concert the newspapers gave us the most wonderful reviews. They compared our kind of music with that of Furtwangler and it was most gratifying because we were the very first dance band ever to play in this famous Concert Hall.

Back in London again, the band continued to tour in variety until the Summer of 1938 when my health broke down again with the return of the ailment that had necessitated my going to Switzerland in 1931 – pleurisy. Once again I was ordered to Switzerland to rest and, of course, it meant disbanding. But as there was no alternative I got on my way and my enforced rest did the trick.

Before returning to England I went to Germany, to the Black Forest where millions of tall trees stretch up and up towards the sky, each straighter than the next, and then all at once you come upon this beautiful small town, Baden-Baden, nestling in the very heart of it, clean and picturesque. In the centre of this lovely holiday resort was a large park housing the casino and smart shops in a sunlit street bordered on each side by leafy trees. Then there was the Stephenie Hotel where I spent very happy times. So much so that I returned to it again, as it offered so many of the things I enjoyed doing in my holiday month of August. That was when I gave the band a break in our strenuous activities each year.

I especially remember 1938 in this quiet and peaceful little place away from all the razzamatazz I encountered in my everyday life of showbusiness. When I arrived at the hotel and registered, I noticed that there were quite a good many German officers dressed in uniform standing talking to smart women, and there was an air of excitement. In just a few minutes I was to know the reason. I did not think much of the incident at the time as the party of officers, who were entering through swinging doors, were saluted with outstretched hands by everyone present who shouted 'Heil!' I noticed that in the midst of this important group, who lost no time reaching the lift, was a rather small man with a small moustache decorating his upper lip, and he seemed to enjoy the fuss the people were making of him and his entourage. I asked the manager who that person was, which rather surprised him. I could tell by his look of utter disgust – and when he told me it was Hitler I could understand why he must have thought I was slightly off my rocker.

During the evening just before making my way to the

casino, I was sitting in the bar with a friend who was very well known in the upper circles, especially the type who frequented that hotel, and as we were talking, a party of five or six officers entered and came over to the bar just next to us. My friend spoke to one of them and asked him to join us for a drink, which he did. The man was rather on the stout side and displayed many medals on his uniform, in fact more medals than I'd ever seen before on one man – but of course I had never seen many soldiers with medals on their chest. His name was Goring. And as my records were very popular in Germany at the time I was not too surprised when Goring told me he had several of them. Had I known how much it was going to cost me in the Casino I'm sure I would have extended my stay at the bar and bought Goring another drink.

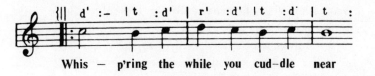

Whis — p'ring the while you cud–dle near

19. Australia

JUST BEFORE I left to return to London, a friend of mine telephoned me from Australia and said a big Palais in Melbourne wanted me to come there to form an Australian band; and the Australian Broadcasting Commission wanted me to do a thrice weekly broadcast called 'Roy Fox's After Dinner Show'. I didn't like the idea much of not returning to London at once, but after talking it over with my doctor, he advised me to accept the offer so that I would escape the winter in London and get a lot of sunshine in Australia before tackling the British climate again so soon. So the outcome was that I found myself on the bandstand of the St Kilda Palais in Melbourne in front of an Australian band of the best musicians one could wish for.

We had an excellent opening night, and I must say the band was really superb. I was rather surprised the Australian boys were such fine players and, aside from the arrangements I had been playing with my British band, there were one or two terrific arrangers in the band. I had five vocalists, all of whom were great, and I had taken Pat McCormack (my Irish singer from England) with me. Then there was Olive Lester, an

Australian girl who was rated the top singer there; plus an American girl and boy who were both first class. All in all, I was proud and happy to have had such luck with the quality of this band. The dancers gave me a wonderful reception and it looked as though everything was going to be just great again. I forgot to mention that as the ship I had arrived in entered the harbour at Melbourne, a small launch drew alongside the ship and we all thought it was customs or someone connected with the docking of the boat. But, much to my surprise, when the men came on board, one of them came to me and asked me if I would mind if they broadcast my arrival from the ship – they were from the Australian Broadcasting Commission. Well, we did a twenty minute live broadcast, which was recorded; and during the nine months I remained in Australia that same record was broadcast nearly every day.

I was very pleased to see the amount of fan mail I received from our 'Roy Fox's After Dinner Show' broadcasts. It was most gratifying to know that the Australian people liked me and the band very much.

With all that terrific sunshine (it was 110 in the shade when I arrived) and plenty of golf, I was beginning to feel like my old self again and everything was 'swinging'.

Then the time came for the renewal of my contract at the Palais (which, incidentally, was very posh on Friday nights – you had to dress to get in and, on account of the rather odd licencing laws, a person had to bring his own bottle), but I thought a tour of the country would be highly rewarding financially, so I prepared an extended journey which would take the band not only to the main cities but to many of the smaller towns too. It's funny how sometimes you just know you're doing the right thing and that was the case with this venture.

After all, with the publicity at the Palais and the tremendous exposure the band had on the air – well, we just couldn't miss. One of the first places we played at was the Annual Ball at Canberra. It being the capital, the Mayor and all of the Government officials were there. They were all there, but Roy Fox and his band weren't. Instead of being on the bandstand at nine o'clock that evening, we were sitting in our special coach in the middle of the road quite some miles from the town. The only difficulty was that it was raining so hard the water was up over the floorboards – and we were stuck.

It wasn't till help came through the kindness of a mule someone had brought to our aid that we finally arrived at the Ball and, on account of being so late, we had to start playing even without a shave or changing into our dress uniform. I didn't have time to don my beautiful tails. I thought it might relieve the tension if we played as our opening tune *It Ain't Going to Rain No More,* but I don't think the Mayor saw the joke.

Well, even that didn't help much, and I can assure you I never felt so uncomfortable standing in front of a band as I was then. And if I had known what was to follow I think I would have stayed in the coach until the water was over my head. What a nightmare that trip was. That rain bit happened on more than one occasion and twice the dance evenings had to be cancelled on account of 'Rain no play'. We just couldn't get there. I've seen it rain hard, but nothing to compare with the downpour they arrange for you in Australia.

Then one day we arrived at a small town which looked just like our 'Western' towns in the States.

The place where we were going to give our concert was a rather small cinema cum entertainment hall. The town had only one main street and while I was changing, my manager came into what was called a dressing-room and told me there were only a few people in the house. As it was nearly time for the show to begin I asked him to get the house manager. This man assured me that he had given our visit the utmost publicity, but the reason we didn't have many people was the fact that just down the street we had 'great opposition'. In my band I had over twenty people and I'm sure no one in Australia had ever had more publicity, so it was a little difficult to imagine just what kind of 'opposition' there could possibly be in a town where there was only one street. The manager explained most clearly that just down the street in an old barn 'Tex somebody' was appearing with his guitar and all the people in the town and out-of-town went to hear him. Now this was an 'Australian' cowboy and it gives you a picture of the type of thing one might run into during those days before the war. So just in remembrance of that incredible cowboy I'd like to say: 'Good on ya.'

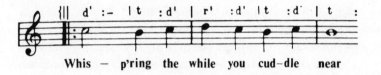

Whis — p'ring the while you cud–dle near

20. The War Years In The States

WELL, AFTER ALL my wonderful expectations, not only was I more than disappointed, but it was starting to cost me money that I didn't have. A friend of mine came to the rescue with the result that it also cost him money. So what was I to do but to scrap the whole idea and come back to London. Soon all my thirty two pieces of luggage were put on the boat to be taken back to what I called home by this time – England. I sent Pat McCormick and Dorothea on ahead as I wanted to fly to Melbourne to see the Melbourne Cup Race before leaving and, while there, I visited the American Consul to thank him for his great kindness. But, as it was 1939 (I had been there nine months), the Consul, when he heard I was on my way back to London, said that on account of the war, which had already started, he would have to cancel my passport. This was because I was still an American citizen and, as America hadn't entered the war as yet, he suggested I get all my luggage off the ship along with Pat and Dorothea and take the first boat back to the States. Eventually that was the way it worked out and I was really broken-hearted. I had lived in Britain for about eight years and everything I had was there, it was my home, but that made no difference. What was I going to do back in the States? The only thing left was to find out.

At least here was the chance to see my mother again and I knew my sister would be glad to have me home after such a long time. I arrived back in Hollywood about Christmas time and it was a very happy home-coming. One of the very first things that happened while I was living at the Beverly Wilshire Hotel in Beverly Hills was to find Ray Noble was playing with his band. Ray had a marvellous American band and we spent some time talking over old times. Then one day my telephone rang and it was Bob Cobb, the proprietor of the Brown Derby restaurants in Hollywood. Bob said he had just heard I had arrived back and invited me to attend a party he was giving. It was the most wonderful party. Jack Benny and many other stars were there and I remember Bob had engaged the most terrific trio to play. Just three musicians, the greatest jazz cello player I had ever heard and two others. This cellist played impossible things and the harp player was out of this world, as well as the guitarist. What music! The room at the Brown Derby at Hollywood and Vine Street, where the party was given, was all made of bamboo and was really sensational. It was nice to see Bob Cobb again after so long a time because I used to know him when he was just the manager of the original Brown Derby opposite the Ambassador Hotel when I played in the Cocoanut Grove. A man by the name of Herb Sonborn (Gloria Swanson's husband) built the Brown Derby and when he died Bob Cobb took over. It seemed a long time ago when I used to go across the street to have some flap-jacks with Bob at about two or three o'clock in the morning.

After living in London for eight years, enjoying the

success I had there, and liking the way of life which appealed to me, then having the hectic and rather disastrous trip I made to Australia, being back in Hollywood seemed quite strange to me. It wasn't the same at all. Yes, I really missed Britain, a long way away at the moment. It was like almost starting all over again. What was the next step? Well, out of a clear blue sky one day I had an offer to go to New York to form a band to open at the famous Rainbow Room in Radio City.

This was most acceptable and a good friend of mine, George Coogan (he was Jackie Coogan's uncle), went to New York with me. George was going to be my personal manager. On the way George told me about a beautiful girl who was in New York named Kay Kimber, who, he said, would be a terrific singer with the band. She had been to Hollywood where she made some films, one being *Dodsworth* with Walter Huston, and while there, she had been chosen as the most beautiful young actress in Hollywood that year. But now she was in a musical in New York called *Two for the Show*, playing the lead. When George and I arrived in New York, we went to see the show; and this was the girl I had to have for the band if I could get her. She was just as pretty as George had said and I could understand why they had chosen her as the most beautiful girl in Hollywood. But when I heard her sing, that settled it! She had a three-and-a-half octave range voice which was really lovely. Her song in the production was *How High the Moon*, which, of course, is still popular today.

When George and I went backstage after the performance Kay was surprised to see him. He introduced me and told her what we were in New York for. She said that, quite by chance, the show was closing the very next week and she would like to join the band for the

Rainbow Room. What terrific news this was, being able to get this girl. As soon as she had changed into street clothes, the three of us went to Lindy's restaurant on Broadway; this was the place I told you I went to with the Marx Brothers when I was in New York earlier. I arranged the deal with Kay and we were all very happy. She was a lovely girl and I liked her very much. It didn't take long for me to find the musicians I wanted for the band and we started our rehearsals. Tommy Rockwell (one of New York's top agents), who had booked my band, came in one day and said: 'Roy, you may as well stop rehearsing because they have decided to close the Rainbow Room.' With the war on it was feared there may be bomb attacks, and it would be especially dangerous in a place where they were dancing practically on top of Radio City. Quite a good many clubs were closed at that time. Well, if one of the bombs had dropped on me, it wouldn't have jarred me any more than this news did. I just couldn't believe that, after all the misfortune I had encountered in Australia, things could still happen like this. But they could, and they did. So, once again, what was I to do? Luckily, Tommy Rockwell came up with something almost immediately; he booked me into La Martinique with my band. It was a well known night-club in the very heart of New York, and the job included a weekly broadcast over the Columbia Network. Luckily this got my name before the public again after so long a time. There was a terrific floor-show at La Martinique which featured big names and there was a young Jewish comedian in the show who had been playing around New York in cabaret for a short time – his name was Danny Kaye. Although he was sensational, he had not yet 'set the world on fire', but people were starting to talk about him. Quite early in life Danny Kaye became an entertainer, dancer and actor on stage, screen and TV, and in time won the plaudits of a worldwide public. He specialised in zany comedy, and was always a very sympathetic personality. During his performance his wife, Sylvia Fine, would sit at the piano and play, for she was his accompanist normally. She also wrote most of the songs he sang.

One night someone came in to hear Danny and they offered him a part in a play called *Lady in the Dark* starring Gertrude Lawrence on Broadway. Danny accepted and overnight he was the new sensation – everyone was talking about him. People flocked to see and hear him at La Martinique and that was really the beginning of his fantastically successful career. And I would like to make a point of saying that Danny and Syvia are two of the nicest people I have ever met. Danny was exactly the same after his great success as he was before and I'm sure he has always remained the same – very, very likeable.

Wednesday night, just as at the Cocoanut Grove in Hollywood, was Celebrity Night at La Martinique. Lots of stars came there to join in the fun. They would get up on the floor and do an act during the special cabaret time. They would be picked out of the audience and the spotlight would focus on them; then everyone would applaud them until they came out to do their stuff. One such person who used to come in quite often was Milton Berle.

Betty Hutton was another star who was very popular with the crowd; the only difficulty when she decided to have a go was that she practically wrecked the microphone every time she got going. I remember the owner nearly having a nervous breakdown each time she touched the mike. She actually wrestled with it. I'm sure you can understand this when I tell you that one of her most famous numbers was *Murder He Says*. She put her heart and soul into it, so much that the bandstand was a shambles when she finished.

Just about the most popular star to get up during one of our Celebrity Nights was Jimmy 'Schnozzle' Durante. He never failed to 'bring the house down' and each time he was there he just had to do one of his numbers at the piano, for he was so well liked. I used to put in telephone calls to Hollywood to Dorothea, who wished to remain there. I suppose by now she found it much more satisfactory not having me around so that she could do her drinking without my trying to help her, which she had grown to resent. I would get reports which caused me a great deal of worry, but that was the way it was and I couldn't do much about it. Much to my surprise, one day I received a notification from Reno stating that she had secured a divorce. Naturally, I was taken aback at this piece of information, even though she had in one of her drunken moments threatened me with this possibility; it really did come as a shock. She had sold some of the diamonds I had given her to make the trip to Reno and finance the whole deal.

I couldn't help wondering what might have happened if this had taken place while I was seeing so much of Jean Harlow. I am certain we would have married, as that was the way it was between us, but Jean had met an untimely death during my absence.

My band was becoming fairly well known by this time and after each broadcast I received a large amount of fan mail. Kay Kimber was also making quite a name for himself over the air but, even though everything was starting to go very well, I was anxious to get back to London. I really missed it and each time anyone came to the club from England, it was wonderful getting news of what was going on. Naturally, it was sad to hear about the war news and what had happened to some of my friends, but that was where I wanted to be.

I stayed at La Martinique for a while, until I had an offer from another new club, the Rio Bamba, which was about to open. It was situated on 57th Street near the East River and was to be very 'swanky'. I accepted the offer and the opening was terrific. In our floor show was . a young singer who had been with the Tommy Dorsey orchestra and also with Harry James – he was making his first appearance in cabaret. I first met him at rehearsal, during which he came over to me after we had accompanied him in a slow number. I expected him to say how much he liked our music. But when he said in no uncertain terms: 'You are probably the lousiest conductor I've had the misfortune of meeting', I, of course, was slightly surprised and asked him what was wrong. He said I hadn't given him the right tempo. We finally got everything straightened out and, as soon as rehearsal was over, I went to his dressing-room and really told. him off. That seemed to do the trick, for Frank Sinatra and I are very good friends. He began as a sports writer, but gave it up to be a singer on radio. When he became a pop star he was admired by millions the world over. In 1943 he went into films, and gave most arresting performances in *From Here to Eternity, Guys and Dolls, High Society, Pal Joey* and many others. I visited him on one of his trips to Britain, and I must say, he certainly 'slayed' the folks at the club. That is when the word 'swoon' was invented. That, in fact, was exactly what happened; the girls were practically falling on their faces, much to their boys friends' annoyance.

Someone I hadn't seen since I was at the Montmartre Cafe appeared in our cabaret – it was Connie Boswell. She was by herself for, I believe, the sister team had broken up by that time. Connie was also sensational with the guests and they would hardly let her leave the floor until she had sung all their old favourites. She was just as good as ever, which was very good indeed. A nice person to remember.

While I was at the Club a good friend of mine came in when he heard that I was playing there and he brought his violin with him. I invited him to 'sit in' and play a tune with the band, and when he started to play I recalled that when he was in California with the Paul Whiteman Orchestra, he used to come to the Montmartre Cafe and 'sit in'. Every time he did that the people would gather around. The same thing was now happening here at the Rio Bamba; all he had to do was to start playing and sure enough, people would stop dancing just to listen. Of course, they were listening to the great Joe Venuti and his jazz fiddle.

At night after my band finished at the club, Kay Kimber and I would sometimes go to a place called Spivy's. It was run by a woman called Spivy and was a very late night spot in a penthouse on top of one of the buildings in the heart of Manhattan. We went there especially to hear a wonderful pianist who used to play different request tunes asked for by the guests. He was quite a good looking guy with an attractive personality. The whole room was lit by candlelight and the atmosphere was just right for his kind of piano playing. Kay and I became quite well acquainted with him and I'm sure we both would have been more than surprised had we known that some day this piano player, who partly existed on the 'tips' he made from the guests, would eventually fare much, much better on the money he made playing for millions of people when he became known as Liberace.

Some nights Kay and I would go down to what was

known as the 'village', that is Greenwich Village, where
there were many really late night joints and you could
hear wonderful music played by jazz groups. One such
place was where Eddie Condon and his gang were
playing. What a swinging bunch of boys he had. We
would sit for hours just listening to them and especially
to Eddie.

But back at the Rio Bamba Frank Sinatra and I were
hitting it off much better than we had done in the
beginning, and there was one song that had been especially written for the baby his wife had just presented
to him. Johnny Mercer, a friend of mine, had composed
it and, as the baby's name was Nancy, Johnny called
the tune *Nancy with the Laughing Face* and Frank really
sang it.

One night my manager, George Coogan, and I went
after work to another club where Josh White was
playing. George and Josh had known each other since
George's nephew, Jackie Coogan, had been in films with
Charlie Chaplin, and it was the first time I had heard
Josh White in person. His singing and playing was so
wonderful that George and I remained after all the
other people had left the club, when Josh sat and sang
and played for just the two of us until daylight. In any
case, that was about the time you would go home in
New York, but this night I shall always remember. You
probably couldn't have paid Josh to do it, but he liked
George so much that he went on and on and seemed to
enjoy it as much as we did.

One day I was walking down Broadway and I passed
Jack Dempsey's Bar and, as I hadn't seen him since I
was working with the Abe Lyman band, I thought I
would go in to see if Jack was there and, sure enough,
he was. When he saw me he asked me to sit down to
have a drink and the first thing he talked about was

way back in those far off days when he used to come to
The Sunset Inn just after he had become World
Champion. We recalled all the stars who used to come
there. Jack, at that time, was married to a film star and
he was saying how much he enjoyed the kind of dance
music we played then. I used to notice he was pretty
light on his feet on the dance floor – maybe it was on
account of the experience he had in the ring getting
around guys like Gene Tunney. About this time I was
propositioned by the Savoy Plaza Hotel, just opposite
Central Park, to take my band there. It was one of the
top hotels in New York City and, needless to say, I
accepted without much hesitation. It was a class place
and catered for a society clientele – 'debs' and all that.
One of the first things that happened after our opening
was the night Peggy Joyce (the girl who never married
anyone but millionaires) came to see me at the Hotel
and she was crying – we went around one summer
holiday when I was in Monte Carlo. She said she had
just left the hotel where Marion Harris had been living
in New York and Marion had burned to death in her
room from a fire caused by a lighted cigarette. This was
a great loss to me as Marion and I had been close
friends and had worked so many places together. A
really wonderful singer and person.

Xavier Cugat had now established himself and his
Latin American music at the Waldorf Astoria Hotel as
the outstanding band for this type of music. He had
built the orchestra up to a very large aggregation and
I have never heard such music. Quite often Xavier
would come to see me at the Savoy Plaza and he would
bring in that tiny little dog you may have seen him
hold in some of his films. That dog (a Chihuahua or
Mexican Hairless) became almost as famous as Cugat's
orchestra. He and I would reminisce about the time he

had his little tango band at the Montmartre Cafe when I was playing there.

I had another good friend, Fred Waring. I had first met him in California but now he was one of the star attractions on radio, playing with his band on the Chesterfield Hour Show. He had a very large band and the most wonderful glee-club you could wish to listen to. Their voices and arrangements were terrific and, to give you just some idea how popular the show was, I understood Fred received around 25,000 dollars *per show*. I remember one week he also played at the Roxy Theatre and he earned a similar amount from the theatre. That was the kind of money a big attraction could make at that time. One day I was with Fred in his office on Broadway and it was all built of bamboo with fish tanks set into the walls and a rehearsal room for the band adjoining the office, with a kitchen alongside. He'd just bought a golf course and an hotel so he was doing all right – that is, in comparison with the time when he had brought his band to the coast and had lost so much money, he couldn't pay his musicians. But he deserved his popularity as his music was the tops.

There was another fine band at the Lincoln Hotel headed by Harry James. What a wonderful trumpet player! Looking back now I believe Harry James was probably the trumpet player I liked best of all. I liked his singing tone and he had great technique. The only thing I didn't like was that when you entered the room in which he was playing you were nearly blown out of the place. But the arrangements were terrific.

One day I received an urgent message to come to California at once as my mother was critically ill. Upon arrival I learned she was suffering from the high blood pressure which had caused more than one stroke.

Luckily she had pulled through on each occasion but, as she had been ill off and on for a number of years, it finally overcame her. The thing I remember most about seeing her lying in bed was when she imagined I was the grocer's boy who had been delivering groceries regularly for quite some time and, as she was in a semi-coma, I sat at her bedside and she told this grocer's boy what a wonderful son her boy, Roy, was. I carried on the conversation with her, not being able to make her understand I had come home to be with her. The end came quietly and sweetly, and never could a boy have a more loving mother.

She was buried in the beautiful Forest Lawn Cemetery and the building which houses her grave is just next to that where Jean Harlow rests. It seems strange to me that two of the people I loved so much should, quite by accident, be so close together.

On my arrival back in New York, one of the New York agents got in touch with me and told me that the Congress Hotel, the largest in Chicago at the time, was interested in having a meeting with me to discuss my band for their Room. So I arranged to take a few days off from the Savoy Plaza, where I was working, and I arrived in Chicago to see what the offer was all about. Some way or other Ben Bernie, a very famous band leader, heard I was in Chicago, and he telephoned to invite me out that evening to see the town. He, at that time, was broadcasting weekly on the Wrigley Hour with his orchestra, and it was his band that followed me into the Montmartre Cafe in Hollywood when I left to go to Fox Films. Ben picked me up later that evening and he came in and said he had a friend of mine waiting in the taxi, so when we went out the cab door was opened by the occupant, Jack Benny. I hadn't seen Jack since the party in Hollywood and it was great to see him again. As it was my first time in Chicago, they took me round the town for a most marvellous time. I couldn't possibly forget that the last place they took me to was a club which featured some of the most beautiful girls I had seen for a long time. They were strictly high class, the very cream of 'strippers' and I don't remember having more laughs than I did that night with Ben Bernie and Jack Benny.

After discussing the offer with the management of the Congress Hotel, I went back to New York to await their decision and no sooner had I arrived than I was asked to appear with my band on what was called the Atlantic Spotlight radio programme. It was a weekly transatlantic two-way series between Britain and America and, on this particular programme, I had my band in the NBC Studios in New York and the great Glenn Miller was in the BBC Studios in London. I opened the show from our end by saying: 'Hello, Ladies and Gentlemen in Britain. This is Roy Fox speaking from New York; and hello Glenn Miller!' Glenn acknowledged it by telling me how much he liked being in Britain and the royal welcome he had received. Then I told him I had a surprise for him and on my opening number I featured his former vocal group 'The Modernaires' and when he heard them he was overjoyed. Naturally, they couldn't be with Glenn in Britain as his band was military and that ruled them out, especially as there was one girl. But they spoke to Glenn over the air and he was really happy to hear their voices wishing him well. And, of course, his wonderful music was unsurpassable.

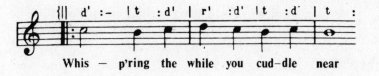

Whis — p'ring the while you cud-dle near

21. London Again

I KNEW DUKE Ellington was playing with his orchestra at a place on Broadway called The Hurricane and so I thought I'd wander in one night to pay him a visit. After all, he had come in to see me at the Kit Kat in London when he was there, so in I went and as soon as the head-waiter told him I was there, he came over to the bar and we had the most wonderful visit. He was the nicest guy, and his band of course was great as usual. The club was packed out every night and when the Duke heard I would be going back to London as soon as I got permission, he asked me if I would like to introduce to the British audience a new number he had just written, which I did over the air on my return there.

By this time Kay Kimber and I had become more than just good friends and were soon married. She liked the idea of returning to England with me (the war was still on and on my arrival from Australia the authorities had cancelled my passport) so in 1943 I thought I would take a trip to Washington to see if I could talk them into letting me have my passport back so that I could return to entertain the British troops as my part of the war effort. I had been turned down, for medical reasons, by the US Army, so I arrived in Washington and applied for the passport and after staying for two days I was happy to learn they would not stop me returning to London. They said I would have to apply in New York for my visa, so back to New York I went and when I went to see the powers-that-be in the British Consulate, they said they were terribly sorry but it was impossible for them to grant my wish. The only alternative was for me to allow them to cable London for permission, which they did at my expense, and in a couple of weeks the answer came – No! They explained that all available space was for military personnel. So my trip to Washington was of no avail. But the closest I came to entertaining the British troops was at a club in the Savoy Plaza exclusively for members of the British Merchant Marine and each night I would take my band upstairs and entertain the boys who had heard me in Britain and it was wonderful talking to some of them about old times. They were so glad to see someone from 'home'. And there was another club in Greenwich Village where I used to take the band to entertain them.

But time finally passed and then I got the okay to return to London. Strangely enough, the very day I received the news, I had an offer to go to the Mount Royal Hotel in Montreal, Canada, to appear with an all Canadian band. I was allowed to take Kay as my vocalist and my New York arranger. The contract was for three years, but I had waited so long to get back to London I just had to forego the offer. It was rather disappointing in a way because the job in Canada would have meant that I would be broadcasting every night from Montreal right through to California on a coast-to-coast hook-up. But within a few weeks I was on the Queen Elizabeth on my way to what I now consider home. Kay was to remain in New York until I had arrived back after getting everything settled in London. On the way over we encountered another terrible storm which compared favourably with the one I told you about on my way from Miami, Florida, to New York.

But I finally arrived back in London and it looked almost as depressing as I had imagined it would. Where my name had appeared in neon lights in front of the Monseigneur in Piccadilly, everything seemed to be so dark and dreary. Naturally, I knew London wouldn't look the way I had left it, but it was a very sad sight indeed. The Press learned I was back again and my name appeared in the papers, giving accounts of what I'd been doing since leaving in 1938 to go to Switzerland. And the very next day John Mills, the proprietor of the Milroy Club in Mayfair, telephoned me and asked me to go to see him. We met and he said that Harry Roy had been playing at the club with his band but they had had a misunderstanding so would I consider forming a band and accept the engagement. This I readily did as I wanted to get rolling again as soon as possible and, before long, I had assembled a good bunch of boys. Then, after rehearsing for a short time, came the opening at the Milroy.

The room was crowded with many of the people I used to play for before the war and when John Mills met me at the door before we started to play, he said someone had asked me to come to their table as soon as I arrived. John took me over to where (much to my surprise) was sitting Marina, The Duchess of Kent, and she smiled and said she just wanted to wish me 'Good Luck' on my return to Britain. She was such a lovely person and it really made me feel wonderful to think she would take the trouble to welcome me back. Jack

Buchanan, of course, was there among several of my friends I hadn't seen since leaving England. It was a most wonderful opening. It seemed just as though I had never left. Jack Nathan and Syd Buckman were in the band again, which helped to make it less strange for me, and I felt lucky to have been able to assemble such a good band because musicians were still being demobbed and there was a bit of a shortage. I still remember that, when the Duchess danced, she asked me to play a tune she liked very much and it sort of took me back to the days when I had first come to London to play at the Cafe de Paris when the Prince of Wales was always there nearly every night accompanied by the Duke of Kent, and I had become quite friendly with both of them. I know the Duchess loved to dance and each time after that opening night at the Milroy, when I saw her enter the room, I would always play her favourite song, *I'll See You Again.*

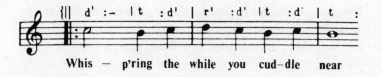

Whis — p'ring the while you cud–dle near

22. Changes

LONDON STARTED TO really 'swing' at that time and I was invited to many cocktail parties and on one occasion I was surrounded by people who wanted to say Hello after not seeing me for so long a time; and once several of the men asked me if I would be interested in opening my own club if they put up the money. This sounded like a pretty good idea, but after searching I decided it was impossible to find the kind of room I wanted, so the whole thing was forgotten.

, By this time my wife, Kay, had joined me here in London and no sooner had she arrived than Jack Hylton, on hearing that she was here and as he had seen her in New York in the musical *Two for the Show,* signed her to star in the new musical he was putting on at the Hippodrome Theatre in London called *High Button Shoes.* Her co-stars were to be Alfred Marks and Sydney James. That was when I first met them. Syd and I used to go fishing at almost every chance we had; he's a great fisherman, and he still enjoyed it even when he didn't have a bite, and that, I might say, was more often than not. At least we had a lot of laughs.

One night Kay introduced me to a lovely young girl

who was a dancer in the chorus. I couldn't help noticing how beautiful she was and when you see her on the screen these days, you will recognise her as Audrey Hepburn.

When Kay's show closed it was about the time I had planned to take the band out on the road again in variety. This is the thing I had waited for since arriving back in Britain, so I arranged to leave the Milroy Club and booked my opening date at West Ham, not a very large theatre but it would do for a 'break-in' week. This was in the winter of 1947 and it is still thought of as the worst winter within memory.

We opened with our new act and if I had shot a shot-gun off in the theatre I wouldn't have hit anyone. The seats were entirely empty, with the exception of just a very few faithful fans who would have braved anything to be on hand. People could hardly get through the streets because of the snow and there was not one bit of heat of any kind. Kay was singing with the band now, and not only was she absolutely frozen in the very flimsy dress she wore, but all the boys in the band could hardly play their instruments. I tried wearing a light jersey under my tails but my suit fitted so well I could hardly get into it. Nothing could make our music sound good; the gang were too cold. Luckily they all tried to make the best of it but it was most difficult to put on a good show when the few persons who did find their way to the theatre had car rugs or blankets over their laps.

Added to this it was my usual custom, as I said earlier, when playing the variety theatres, to play on a percentage – that is, I would take a certain percentage of the box office takings and I would be responsible for the payment of the acts on the bill. With the salaries of the band, plus the acts, I was stuck for the entire salary list and that amounted to several hundreds of pounds. Unfortunately, I didn't have hundreds of pounds on hand and was depending on getting it by playing theatres again as I used to. But alas, the freeze up continued, then continued some more. All this time, of course, I was losing money which I had to borrow. Naturally, it ran into a few thousand and I could not see any let up. It was starting to remind me of the old gag about the bookmaker who kept losing money night after night and his friend asked him why he didn't quit and the bookie said: 'It is my living'. But it wasn't funny at this point.

The only answer was to give it a miss, so what was my next move? Then one evening I was sitting in my flat and the telephone rang and Kay said it was someone from the Isle of Man wanting to speak to me. The voice at the other end said he was connected with the Palace Company on the Island and would it be possible for me to open with my band in about a month's time at the Palace Ballroom for a seventeen week season. I didn't want to tell the voice just what a nice voice it was, but the more we talked about money the sweeter it became.

He told me he would have to have a chat with the committee to discuss the money I was asking (I had to ask a lot), and later that night he was on the 'phone again accepting my proposition. That was a real god-send, just when I did not know quite what was going to happen. How was I going to repay all the money I had borrowed? But here was my chance.

At this point I must explain that I had another item in the back of my mind which was always with me, in the form of a little note I received from the Income Tax Department in Britain when I was still living in New York. When I saw the envelope I wondered why they were getting in touch with me. My tax had been paid weekly to my accountants in London up to the time I left for Switzerland. It had been paid up to date. You can imagine my surprise when I opened the letter telling me that there was a sum owing for surtax to the tune of a little less than ten thousand pounds.

After my sojourn in Australia and the result of that disaster, the idea of owing this amount of cash to the British Government did not appeal to me. I knew it was all a mistake, but it wasn't! Upon my arrival back in London, it was very simply pointed out to me how this money was owed, quite unbeknown to me. So you may understand, with that still on my plate, plus the added borrowed money to think about, the money I would be earning at the Isle of Man would be most handy. And with the exception of living expenses, it all went toward the repayment of the tax and the loans.

One thing I have always found to be a sure cure for any difficulty of this nature was to get on to a golf course and take it out on the ball. This I did practically every day for the entire seventeen weeks we spent on the Isle of Man. Often Kay would play too – it was a glorious summer. Hardly a cloud in the sky. We had a lovely house and if it hadn't been for the constant money problem, it could have been ideal. But one thing I was beginning to notice, the Palace could accommodate around eleven thousand dancers. On the TT races night I have never seen so many people on a dance floor, but on other nights I felt there should be more people dancing to our music.

This went on all summer and it seemed strange to see so many very young kids dancing. Some of them appeared to be only about fifteen years old and I noticed on one side of the bandstand that there were a bunch of them and they would request 'bop' music, while on the other side of the rostrum the kids would ask for 'trad', while all this time the people who had danced to Roy Fox and his music before the war were wondering what was happening to Roy Fox. The answer was, I was trying to please the kids (both kinds) and everyone else, all at the same time, and it wasn't working.

A lot of the teenagers by this time had never heard of Roy Fox and his Band. A war had intervened. Their Mums and Dads knew, but they weren't going out so much nowadays. There was some sort of a change I didn't quite understand. They were even starting to dance differently.

The same thing was taking place everywhere we played after leaving the Isle of Man. We weren't playing to nearly as many people as I had in these same places before the war. Then you couldn't get near the place; but it wasn't so now. Kay, although she was a most wonderful person, wasn't enjoying this kind of life very much – she was beginning to miss the States and especially her family in Iowa where she came from. But I assured her it wouldn't always be like this; things just had to turn better, and everything then would be like old times again. But I had an inward feeling that I was crying in the wind! There was distinctly something radically wrong. Something had to be done about it. I must try and forget touring around the country, losing even more money than I had before.

So I wondered what Ireland was like in those days. I had been there with the band several times in the past and had always done very well. I got on the 'phone to Louis Elleman who owned the Theatre Royal in Dublin, and made him a proposition whereby I would produce the stage shows at the Royal and conduct a stage band made up of Irish musicians. It was a very large cinema, in which I had played before the war. He accepted my offer and I disbanded my British band, and Kay and I arrived in Dublin a short time after.

I was hoping the change of scenery would help Kay forget about going back home, and it did for a while, but the thought of not being able to see her family and friends proved just too much and one day she told me she had decided to return to America. She said she had given it a lot of thought and although she realized that Britain meant so much to me, she must go back and have the chance to choose between here and the States. She pointed out just how much better off she thought we would be over there, and her arguments made a lot of sense. But somehow I was unable to bring myself to the point of leaving with her. We agreed that she should have the chance of going back and making up her mind for herself. I knew that having to start all over again in America after being in England for so long a time would mean there was a great chance that things might be even more disastrous than trying to work things out here where I was so well known. So off she went with the promise that she would let me have her decision as soon as possible. This of course was something I hadn't planned on and it couldn't have come at a worse time. But I didn't want her to be unhappy staying on here with me when I honestly realized that her every thought was with her family in Iowa. In each letter I received from her I surmised it was only a matter of time before I would be getting word from her that she had chosen to remain there. In the meantime not only were there the rehearsals for the orchestra for which I had taken my own arranger from London, but I had also to start dreaming up ideas for stage productions, which had to be changed weekly. I must say I was given every assistance for any production numbers I planned; and I was asked to attend a radio show at Radio Eireann in Dublin where I heard a terrific young Irish singer called Rose Brennan, whom I signed to join me at the Theatre Royal.

The management of the Theatre Royal were always arranging different publicity stunts for me, and there was one especially I like to remember. On this occasion I was asked to judge the annual Beauty Contest (the same one in which Maureen O'Hara had been chosen the winner a couple of years before), and when it came to selecting the most outstandingly beautiful girl of the year, I thought the organizers had made a very wise choice when they asked me to do the honours. I can truthfully say that when it comes to picking just one winner from all those pretty Irish colleens, a fellow has to keep his mind on what is at hand and, in my case, it took quite a bit of doing. But finally the winners were selected and there was much happiness for some and tears for others.

It was the usual practice of the Theatre Royal to have the Contest winners appear at the Royal during the week following the judging and it fell on . my shoulders to interview each of the three lovely girls on the stage at each performance. This was a most pleasant undertaking on my part and during that week Eileen O'Donnell (who had been acting at the Abbey Theatre in Dublin) and I became quite friendly. She was very young and was happy and gay, and so naturally beautiful with roses in her cheeks and a smile that was so enchanting, you just had to like her. Maybe that is why I had no trouble at all forcing myself to be in her company every time I had the chance. Since Kay had decided to go to the States, I had been very lonesome and I welcomed this opportunity of being with such a nice person.

It was very refreshing talking to this girl who had come from a small village in Southern Ireland – Cashel in County Tipperary. Then one day I received a letter from Kay saying that if I did not return to the States at once, she would apply for a divorce. I thought it most unreasonable for her to make this request for she knew that my future lay in England when we got married in New York, so I thought it only fair I let her know I had no intention of returning to America. The outcome was that she finally secured a divorce and remarried.

My engagement at the Theatre Royal expired and I decided that as I had received so much publicity at the Royal I should take advantage of it by making a tour of Ireland, both North and South. It was a very good band that I took on the road and we played many of the small towns. As a matter of fact, I do not believe there had been an Irish band of its type ever to tour Ireland as to size or quality. Rose Brennan and three other vocalists, including Pat MacCormack, were with me and for some unaccountable reason practically the same thing happened to me as I had encountered in Australia.

What was happening to me? First the illness which sent me to Switzerland for the second time, and the trip to Australia, where just everything went wrong, and then the ups and downs in the States on my arrival back there because of the war in Europe and after all that now it was this! It was the exact opposite from the early days of my career when everything I did was right. When I started to climb the ladder of success each step I took was a new, wonderful adventure and everything I attempted came off -- then finally making the grade, arriving at heights I never even dreamed may be the reward of a lot of hard work. This lasted for several years, but now it was as though someone had pulled the ladder out from under me. It was much quicker on the way down. And not nearly so much fun.

But what was it going to be this time? Back in London, of course, but what then? I talked it over with Eileen O'Donnell and that seemed to be the only solution. She promised she would join me after I got organized, so back I went to get still another band together. I must say, I was extremely lucky to get such a marvellous bunch of young musicians. After much rehearsing we opened on the road and played many of the same places where I had always been so successful. But there was something decidedly wrong! The people were not showing up at our dances and it was an entirely new public. I was still finding the same thing happening – the few Roy Fox 'faithfuls' came to dance to the kind of music they knew so well from the past and wondered what had taken the place of the old Fox style as, once again, I was trying to find out what kind of music was actually wanted by the mixed type of people who did come to see and hear us.

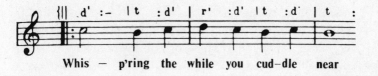

Whis — p'ring the while you cud–dle near

23. Now

DURING THIS TIME Eileen came over to London and we got married and, if it hadn't been for her, things would have been almost unbearable. But being one of the most wonderful persons I have had the good fortune to meet, she helped me to carry on until it became no longer possible. But when things couldn't be more worrying, the most wonderful thing happened; Eileen presented me with a son. We called him Gary and with a girl like Eileen and now this fine baby, things weren't so bad after all. They made the loss of the money I had grown used to having and the Rolls Royces and nice houses which I thought were all part of life seem not quite so important. And never once did Eileen ever complain when things were slightly tough. And they were, plenty of times.

Well, when you have a son you start thinking about the future much more than you generally do and I knew I had to realize that band-leading was just not for me any more. I discovered that what had worked in the thirties had not been successful for me during the forties and fifties. So I disbanded in 1953.

The sad news that the Duke of Windsor had passed

away was, to me, the ending of an era which had always meant so much to me. Since the very first time he came up to me at the Cafe de Paris on my opening night in 1930 to request his favourite tune *Without A Song,* and the friendly way he spoke to me – then, of course, he was the Prince of Wales, the style setter. What the Prince wore, everyone wore. I always paid particular attention to his clothes. If he wore a single-breasted waistcoat with his tails, then I did. The men-about-town always followed suit. It could have been only yesterday that I was asked to appear with the band at a Royal Command Performance at the New Victoria Cinema, which the Prince was to attend. That was in 1933 – over forty years ago – but the memory is as fresh as on the night it all happened. Then when I heard he was to be married at the Chateau de Conde in Tours, France (the Chateau belonged to a very good friend of mine, Charles Bedeaux, so I sort of felt I had a personal interest in the wedding). And the time in Budapest when I met the Prince and his Duchess-to-be at the hotel on the Danube in which we were both staying, and the excitement of the staff in the little restaurant while they were setting the table by candle light with their finest gold service especially for 'the little Prince'. Those are the days I prefer to remember – days when they wrote great melodies like *Without A Song.*

King's Road – that's where I live now – King's Road, Chelsea. Strangely enough, it has the very same flavour about it that Hollywood Boulevard had in the very early days. Days when it was a most glamorous place, where if you were lucky you could see your favourite movie star going shopping or maybe having lunch at one of the ultra-smart restaurants. That, of course, was when a glimpse of these wonderful 'make-believe' people would set your heart alight; just to think, you had actually seen the girl of your dreams. And I'm sure many a sweet young girl's heart nearly stopped at the sight of Valentino coming out of his tailors.

Many a time I can remember heads turning (including mine) when a starlet strode down the Boulevard in the new and rather sexy 'slacks'. These caused much consternation among certain groups who did not think the display of a beautiful girl's backside was quite the thing that should be allowed in public. I may add that a large percentage of these dissenters were women – mostly with very large posteriors. I believe most men rather thought these 'slacks' gave women more freedom and were not a bad idea at all. But in King's Road, the very same thing happened when the new mini-skirts and 'hot-pants' found their way on to some of the prettiest exponents of what it takes to turn a head (including mine), and now and then I hear detrimental remarks like 'What next?' This has been going on as long as I can remember. I hope the day never comes when I agree with them!

But there is always an atmosphere of excitement along the street where some of the most peculiar people gather. Even my son, Gary, sometimes seems to be able to find the strangest ensemble anyone can dream up. Nothing, of course, matches and his hair gets longer each day, but I have to be careful about mentioning the fact, as he may think it is a matter of jealousy, in as much as I lost a fair amount of my hair at an early age. But Chelsea is a great place to live in for someone like me. It's sort of the nerve centre of show-business – actors, film directors and producers, and all kinds of weird human beings.

Well – I don't think you would be terribly interested in the rest of my story. It isn't all that exciting – rather dull in fact compared with the things I've been telling you about. But now and then an echo from those days comes in my direction, as when a major film company propositioned me to appear on the stage of one of the West End cinemas with a band at the premier of one of their pictures. They thought my kind of music would lend atmosphere to the film about the thirties. Then on my last birthday I appeared on four interview programmes where we played some of my recordings and talked about the 'good old days'.

Recently I have been approached by the BBC to appear at a concert at the Royal Festival Hall conducting a large dance band and I feel certain that if I were to accept, it could be the beginning of where I left off. I am convinced that at this moment in time, keeping in mind the amount of fan mail I still receive from different parts of the world, *plus* the nostalgic trend not only in dance music but in dress and in many other ways, I could create an interest in my kind of music once more. I base this on the fact that not so long ago the BBC told me that the teenagers are asking for my records and several polls have been taken over the radio to decide the most popular band of the thirties in which my band received around 85 per cent of the entire vote. This was told to me by two different disc jockeys.

Added to this I have a letter from a Television Director expressing his thanks for my appearance in his production 'It Looks Familiar'. He said that I would probably be pleased to learn that of all the requests received from the public for personalities to appear on the show, the name of Roy Fox has turned up in approximately 85 per cent of the letters received. Another thing that tells me that some kind of change is badly needed in the way of popular music is that a couple of weeks ago the Canadian Television people sent a team of technicians, including a producer, director, camera crew and Elwood Glover, one of the top comperes in Canadian TV. I believe he has the leading 'talk' show. Well, the idea was for them to televise the top people in show business in Britain, allowing each person ten minutes to tell his story. When I had talked for a while recounting some of my experiences, Elwood turned to the cameras and said that although the usual time allotted to everyone was ten minutes, he felt that my story was so interesting that he was going to continue. The outcome of this was that I was allowed to reminisce for half an hour.

In all cases it seems to me that if there is still that amount of interest in me, then there surely must be a public waiting for the kind of music that basically appeals to so many people all over the world. When I say 'all over the world', it is gratifying to know that for the past year I have had a weekly radio series called 'Roy Fox Remembers' being broadcast in South Africa and Australia, and now I have just sold fifty two programmes to Hong Kong where it goes out twice weekly. Each time I tell a story about some of the stars you have been reading about, I play a recording of theirs, even to the very first record I ever made in about 1922 in the States. The interest in this series shown by the English-speaking Chinese, aside from the South Africans and Australians, through their letters, proves to me that my kind of music is still appreciated everywhere.

Not so long ago I was contacted by one of London's leading hotel managements asking me to return to the West End with my band, playing the very same kind of music which used to pack the night clubs. Evening dress is a 'must' instead of the 'no tie' scene which is so prevalent these days. Don't get me wrong – some of the groups are excellent, but I really believe the public is ready for some honest to goodness melody and quiet rhythm, something not only pleasing to listen to but easy to dance to.

I mention all this, realizing I may never take advantage of the offers I get now and then, but just to say that, more than anything, I truly appreciate the fact that so many people still remember what I did so many years ago in the world of dance music. It is rather nice to know that a certain amount of happiness was created by my band's efforts, especially when it happened so long ago and it seems now as though it never really happened at all. When I hear one of my records being played on the radio or on a TV programme, it could be just one of the many bands I have heard in the past – certainly not mine. You see, I am so engrossed in being a Personal Manager these days, helping actors 'make the grade' in television and films, that I seldom think back to the days when I was on the exciting merry-go-round called show business. But unfortunately my 'gold ring' has lost some of its glitter.

So how do you write the last page of a story which has taken a whole lifetime to put together? A lifetime that fills one small book? But every moment of each page has been spent in a world of incredible excitement and I sincerely hope also in giving people a certain amount of enjoyment listening to my music.

It has all been a great joy to me. So looking back what does it all add up to? Success, fame, lots of money, not so much money, good times and bad times, lovely beautiful women, lovely beautiful music, fast beautiful cars and slow beautiful horses (much too slow); but what a wonderfully lucky guy I have been! What a lot of fun every single note has given me – all of which started when a little eleven year old boy, quite by chance, just happened to look into the window of a second-hand store. . . .